Relapse Prevention Counseling Workbook

Practical Exercises for
Managing High-risk Situations

By **Terence T. Gorski** with **Arthur B. Trundy**

Project Team: Terence T. Gorski, Arthur B. Trundy, Steven F. Grinstead, Joseph E. Troiani, and Roland Williams

Based on the GORSKI-CENAPS® Model

Better Treatment, for More People, at a Lower Cost

Dedication

This book is dedicated to Terence Joseph (TJ) Gorski and Nika Gorski who have given me insight into my yesterday and a great new vision for my tomorrow.

Proprietary Information

Produced by The CENAPS Corporation
13194 Spring Hill Drive
Spring Hill, FL 34609
Phone: (352) 596-8000
Fax: (352) 596-8002
E-mail: *info@cenaps.com*

Herald Publishing House/Independence Press
1001 W. Walnut St.
Independence, MO 64050-3562
Phone: 1-800-767-8181 or (816) 521-3015
Fax: (816) 521-3066
Website: *www.relapse.org*

For professional guides and recovery workbooks call 1-800-767-8181 or visit *www.relapse.org*.
Updated clinical materials are available at Terry Gorski's Clinical Development website: *www
.tgorski.com*. Network with other users of this material at *www.relapse.net*.

Training Contact
For training information contact: The CENAPS Corporation (352) 596-8000 or e-mail *info@
cenaps.com*.

Table of Contents

© Terence T. Gorski, 2000. *Relapse Prevention Counseling Workbook—Practical Exercises for Managing High-risk Situations*, Herald Publishing House/ Independence Press, 1-800-767-8181 or (816) 521-3015; Website *www.relapse.org*. Training and Consulation available from The CENAPS Corporation, Phone: (352) 596-8000; Fax: (352) 596-8002; Website: *www.cenaps.com*; E-mail: *info@cenaps.com*.

The Goals of This Workbook

This workbook is designed for people who want to recover from chemical dependency or the use of other self-defeating behaviors. Although this workbook will be of special help to people who have relapsed in the past, all recovering people will benefit from improving their skills at recognizing and effectively managing high-risk situations.

Learning how to manage high-risk situations will require more than just reading this workbook and filling out the exercises. You'll need to discuss your responses to each of the exercises with other people who can help you sort out the thoughts and feelings that get stirred up. We strongly recommend that one of these people be a therapist or counselor trained in the CENAPS® Model of Relapse Prevention. You can get a list of Certified Relapse Prevention Specialists by calling or writing to The CENAPS Corporation, 13194 Spring Hill Drive, Spring Hill, FL 34609, (352) 596-8000 or by visiting their website at *www.cenaps.com* or *www.relapse.org*.

If you are stuck anywhere in the process you can go to our website: *www.cenaps.com* and post your questions on our treatment bulletin board. Many of our certified relapse prevention specialists routinely check the bulletin board and respond to questions. You can also share your experience and insight with others.

If you don't have a therapist, you can do these exercises with the assistance of a self-help group sponsor who is willing and able to support you through this process. It's also a good idea to supplement your individual sessions with group sessions where each member is working through these exercises at the same time. *Discussing what you're learning from each exercise with another person or a group of people will improve your ability to change in a way that will prevent relapse.*

Here are the exercises this workbook will lead you through:

Exercise #1: Making the Commitment to Stop Using

This exercise will guide you through the process of listing the problems that forced you into recovery, identifying the relationship of each of those problems to your alcohol and drug use, determining what will happen with each problem if you keep using alcohol or other drugs, making a conscious commitment to stop using, and signing an Abstinence and Recovery Contract that puts into writing the commitments you are making to yourself about recovery and relapse prevention.

Exercise #2: Planning to Stop Relapse Quickly if It Occurs

In this exercise you will answer three basic questions that will help you stop a relapse quickly should it occur: These questions are: (1) What are you, as a recovering person, going to do to get back in recovery if you start using alcohol or other drugs and decide to stop using before you hit bottom? (2) What is your therapist or counselor supposed to do if you relapse, stop coming to sessions, or fail to honor your treatment commitments? (3) What are the significant people in your life, who support your recovery, supposed to do if you relapse? By answering these questions in detail you will be able to develop an effective plan for stopping relapse before serious problems develop.

Exercise #3: Identifying High-risk Situations

In this exercise you will learn what a high-risk situation is, review a list of the common high-risk situations that can cause relapse, and identify and clarify the immediate high-risk situations that could cause you to use alcohol or drugs despite your commitment not to do so.

© Terence T. Gorski, 2000. *Relapse Prevention Counseling Workbook—Practical Exercises for Managing High-risk Situations*, Herald Publishing House/ Independence Press, 1-800-767-8181 or (816) 521-3015; Website *www.relapse.org*. Training and Consulation available from The CENAPS Corporation, Phone: (352) 596-8000; Fax: (352) 596-8002; Website: *www.cenaps.com*; E-mail: *info@cenaps.com*.

Exercise #4: Mapping and Managing High-risk Situations

In this exercise you will learn what a situation map is and how to develop situation maps for three different kinds of high-risk situations: (1) a past high-risk situation that ended in alcohol or drug use, (2) a past high-risk situation that ended without using alcohol or drugs, and (3) a high-risk situation that you will be facing in the near future. The most important skill that you will learn is how to identify specific points at the beginning, near the middle, and at the end of each high-risk situation where you can do something different to prevent yourself from using alcohol or drugs. You will also explore responsible ways to avoid certain high-risk situations so you won't need to manage them.

Exercise #5: Managing Personal Reactions to High-risk Situations

In this exercise you will learn how to identify the irrational thoughts, unmanageable feelings, self-destructive urges, and self-defeating behaviors that drive you to use alcohol and other drugs. You will also learn how to develop new habits of thinking, managing your feelings and urges, self-regulating your behaviors, and relating to other people in a way that will allow you to manage your high-risk situations.

Exercise #6: Developing a Recovery Plan

In this exercise you will learn how to create a habitual style of living that both minimizes your exposure to high-risk situations and supports you in effectively managing the high-risk situations that you do encounter. This is done by learning about the most effective recovery activities, developing a personal schedule of recovery activities, and using a daily plan. The daily and weekly schedules of recovery activities should support your ongoing identification and effective management of high-risk situations. You will also develop behavioral guidelines for using your new ways of thinking, managing your feelings and urges, behaving and relating to others in each of these scheduled activities.

Exercise #7: Evaluating High-risk Situation Management Skills

In this exercise you will complete a self-assessment of your ability to use the six basic high-risk management skills. You will be asked to evaluate the following areas: (1) the strength of your current commitment to stop using alcohol and others drugs; (2) the effectiveness of your plan to stop relapse quickly should it occur; (3) your ability to identify high-risk situations; (4) your ability to map and manage high-risk situations; (5) your ability to change your personal responses to high-risk situations by effectively managing your thoughts, feelings, urges, actions, and social responses; and (6) your ability to develop and maintain a schedule of recovery activities that support your new and more effective way of managing high-risk situations.

Learning to identify and manage high-risk situations is not easy. It will require hard work and a willingness to use each exercise in this workbook as a tool for self-examination and self-change. It will also require you to develop a schedule of recovery activities and to actively involve other people in your recovery and relapse prevention process. You can recover. Learning how to manage high-risk situations will help.

© Terence T. Gorski, 2000. *Relapse Prevention Counseling Workbook—Practical Exercises for Managing High-risk Situations*, Herald Publishing House/ Independence Press, 1-800-767-8181 or (816) 521-3015; Website *www.relapse.org*. Training and Consulation available from The CENAPS Corporation, Phone: (352) 596-8000; Fax: (352) 596-8002; Website: *www.cenaps.com*; E-mail: *info@cenaps.com*.

Exercise #1: Making the Commitment to Stop Using

In this exercise we are going to ask you to make an honest commitment to stop using alcohol or other drugs for a specified period of time. Because we are asking you for an honest commitment, we want you to see that it is in your best interest to stop.

To help you decide if you want to make the commitment to stop, we are going to ask you to complete a four-part exercise.

First, in *Exercise 1-1* we will ask you to develop a list of problems that motivated you to enter treatment.

Then, in *Exercises 1-2* and *1-3* we will ask you to select the two most important problems and clarify the relationship of each problem to your alcohol and drug use. We will also ask you to think about the best, worst, and most likely thing that could happen in each of those problems if you keep using alcohol and drugs.

Then, in *Exercise 1-4* we will ask you for an honest commitment to stop using alcohol and drugs for a specific period of time. We will also ask you to set up a monitoring and accountability system to back up that decision. This often includes random and on-request testing for alcohol and other drugs.

Finally, in *Exercise 1-5* we are going to ask you to sign a written Abstinence and Treatment Contract that puts into writing the commitments you are making to yourself about recovery and relapse prevention. This agreement clarifies exactly what you are making a commitment to do. We ask you to carefully review this document and take the commitment that you are making seriously. When you sign this agreement you are putting your personal integrity on the line.

Go to the next page and complete Exercise 1-1.

© Terence T. Gorski, 2000. *Relapse Prevention Counseling Workbook—Practical Exercises for Managing High-risk Situations*, Herald Publishing House/ Independence Press, 1-800-767-8181 or (816) 521-3015; Website *www.relapse.org*. Training and Consulation available from The CENAPS Corporation, Phone: (352) 596-8000; Fax: (352) 596-8002; Website: *www.cenaps.com*; E-mail: *info@cenaps.com*.

Exercise 1-1: The List of Problems Forcing You into Treatment

1. List the three most important problems forcing you into treatment at this time. Place a check mark in front of the most important problem.

   ☐ (1) _____

   _____

   ☐ (2) _____

   _____

   ☐ (3) _____

   _____

2. List three problems that, if they were solved to your satisfaction, would significantly improve your life. Place a check mark in front of the most important problem.

   ☐ (1) _____

   _____

   ☐ (2) _____

   _____

   ☐ (3) _____

   _____

In answering the questions below, write both a title (a short word or phrase that describes the problem) and a description (one or two complete sentences that clearly explains what the problem is).

3. Write the most important problem that forced you into treatment. (Refer to your answer to question 1 above.)

   Title: _____

   Description: _____

4. Write the most important thing that could significantly improve your life if you could change it to your satisfaction. (Refer to your answer to question 2 above.)

   Title: _____

   Description: _____

   _____

   _____

Go to the next page and complete Exercise 1-2.

© Terence T. Gorski, 2000. *Relapse Prevention Counseling Workbook—Practical Exercises for Managing High-risk Situations*, Herald Publishing House/ Independence Press, 1-800-767-8181 or (816) 521-3015; Website *www.relapse.org*. Training and Consulation available from The CENAPS Corporation, Phone: (352) 596-8000; Fax: (352) 596-8002; Website: *www.cenaps.com*; E-mail: *info@cenaps.com*.

Exercise 1-2: Problem Analysis Worksheet #1

1. Write the title of the problem that you identified in question 3 of the preceding exercise (The Problem List).

   _____

2. Describe how that problem is related to alcohol and drug use.

   _____

   _____

   _____

   _____

   _____

3. If you continue use of alcohol or drugs...

   A. What is the best thing that could happen to you as a result of this problem?

   _____

   _____

   _____

   _____

   B. What is the worst thing that could happen to you as a result of this problem?

   _____

   _____

   _____

   _____

   C. What is the most likely thing that will probably happen to you as a result of this problem?

   _____

   _____

   _____

   _____

Go to the next page and complete Exercise 1-3.

© Terence T. Gorski, 2000. *Relapse Prevention Counseling Workbook—Practical Exercises for Managing High-risk Situations*, Herald Publishing House/ Independence Press, 1-800-767-8181 or (816) 521-3015; Website *www.relapse.org*. Training and Consulation available from The CENAPS Corporation, Phone: (352) 596-8000; Fax: (352) 596-8002; Website: *www.cenaps.com*; E-mail: *info@cenaps.com*.

Exercise 1-3: Problem Analysis Worsheet #2

1.   Write the title of the problem you identified in question 4 of the preceding exercise (The Problem List).

_____

2.   Describe how that problem is related to alcohol and drug use.

_____

_____

_____

_____

_____

3   If you continue use of alcohol or drugs...

   A. What is the best thing that could happen to you as a result of this problem?

_____

_____

_____

_____

   B. What is the worst thing that could happen to you as a result of this problem?

_____

_____

_____

_____

   C. What is the most likely thing that will probably happen to you as a result of this problem?

_____

_____

_____

Go to the next page and complete Exercise 1-4.

© Terence T. Gorski, 2000. *Relapse Prevention Counseling Workbook—Practical Exercises for Managing High-risk Situations*, Herald Publishing House/ Independence Press, 1-800-767-8181 or (816) 521-3015; Website *www.relapse.org*. Training and Consulation available from The CENAPS Corporation, Phone: (352) 596-8000; Fax: (352) 596-8002; Website: *www.cenaps.com*; E-mail: *info@cenaps.com*.

Exercise 1-4: Deciding What to Do

1. After reviewing your responses to *Exercises 1-1, 1-2, and 1-3*, are you willing to make a commitment to stop using alcohol and other drugs at least for the duration of your treatment?

   ☐ Yes   ☐ No   ☐ Unsure   *Explain your answer:*

   _____

   _____

   _____

2. What are the two most important problems or situations that could make you want to use alcohol or other drugs despite your commitment not to? (We will call these problems or situations *high-risk situations.*)

   High-risk situation #1: _____

   _____

   _____

   _____

   • *How confident are you in your ability to manage this situation without using alcohol or other drugs?*
     (10 = Very Confident; 0 = Not Confident at all) _____

   High-risk situation #2: _____

   _____

   _____

   _____

   • *How confident are you in your ability to manage this situation without using alcohol or other drugs?*
     (10 = Very Confident; 0 = Not Confident at all) _____

3. Are you willing to make a commitment to learn how to manage these high-risk situations by completing a special counseling process?

   ☐ Yes   No   ☐ Unsure   *Explain your answer:*

   _____

   _____

   _____

   _____

   _____

   _____

   _____

   _____

Go to the next page and complete Exercise 1-5.

© Terence T. Gorski, 2000. *Relapse Prevention Counseling Workbook—Practical Exercises for Managing High-risk Situations*, Herald Publishing House/ Independence Press, 1-800-767-8181 or (816) 521-3015; Website *www.relapse.org*. Training and Consulation available from The CENAPS Corporation, Phone: (352) 596-8000; Fax: (352) 596-8002; Website: *www.cenaps.com*; E-mail: *info@cenaps.com*.

Exercise 1-5: The Abstinence and Treatment Contract

Developed by Terence T. Gorski with Tim Dworniczek and Arthur B. Trundy. Revised May 2000.

I, _____ do hereby agree to the following
terms and conditions of treatment.

1. **Abstinence:** I agree to ABSTAIN from using alcohol and mood-altering drugs as long as
   I am receiving service from _____.The term "drug" as used here
   includes any prescribed or non-prescribed mood-altering chemicals (either legal or il-
   legal) that I may use without informing and gaining the consent of my counselor.

2. **High-Risk Situations:** I agree to immediately tell my counselor about any problems or
   situations that may develop during my treatment that could cause me to start using
   alcohol or drugs despite my commitment not to use drugs or alcohol.

3. **Cravings or Urges to Use:** I agree to immediately discuss any cravings or urges to use
   mood-altering chemicals with my counselor.

4. **Desire to Stop Treatment:** I agree to immediately discuss any thoughts or feelings I
   may have about wanting to stop coming to treatment sessions or stop participating in
   other recovery activities such as self-help groups.

5. **Self-reporting of Relapse:** I agree that if I do start using alcohol or drugs I will immediately
   report it to my therapist. After reporting my relapse to my counselor, the following will
   happen: (1) My current treatment plan will be immediately suspended; (2) I will be asked
   to complete a new evaluation to determine what treatment is necessary to stop the relapse;
   (3) I will be given a treatment recommendation (that may include referral for detoxifica-
   tion, residential treatment, or participation in a more intensive or extended outpatient
   program); (4) If I refuse the recommendation, I will be terminated from treatment.

6. **Getting Caught Using:** I understand that if I am caught using alcohol or drugs before I
   report my relapse to my counselor, I will be offered referral for immediate detoxifica-
   tion. If I refuse the referral, I will be immediately terminated from treatment. If I accept the referral, I will be allowed to set up a new screening interview. It will be my
   responsibility to demonstrate in the evaluation session that I recognize what caused
   my relapse and my attempts to hide it and that I am willing to make an honest ef-
   fort to work on resolving those problems. I understand that because of the dishonesty
   involved in my attempts to hide the relapse, the treatment program will exercise a high
   degree of suspicion during this evaluation. It will be up to me to clearly demonstrate
   my motivation and willingness to change.

7. **Alcohol and Drug Testing:** I agree to submit to alcohol and drug testing on a random
   basis and at the discretion of the clinical staff. I understand that my refusal to submit
   to a breath, urine, hair, or other required test will be interpreted as an admission that I
   have been using alcohol or drugs but refuse to admit it.

8. **Prescribed Medications:** I will consult with treatment program staff regarding the use
   of any medications prescribed to me by a physician. I will follow the recommendations
   of the assigned medical doctor of the treatment program regarding the use of any and
   all mood-altering or painkilling medication.

_____ _____ _____ _____
Signature of Client   Date   Signature of Witness   Date

This exercise stops here.

Exercise 2: Planning to Stop Relapse Quickly if It Occurs

One of the goals of completing the *Relapse Prevention Counseling (RPC) Workbook* is to prepare you to stop using alcohol and other drugs quickly if you do start using. This process is called developing a relapse intervention plan.

One of the goals of completing the *Relapse Prevention Counseling (RPC) Workbook* is to prepare you to stop using alcohol and other drugs quickly if you do start using. This process is called developing a relapse intervention plan.

The chances that you will recognize the seriousness of a relapse and take the steps necessary to stop drinking and drugging are dramatically increased if you have already prepared a written plan for what to do. If you have never taken the time or energy to develop a relapse intervention plan, your chances of being able to stop before experiencing serious or life-threatening problems are slim to none.

There are some simple guidelines you can use for developing a plan to stop a relapse quickly should it occur:

1. Never tell yourself, "If I take one drink or one dose of a drug I will lose control and not be able to stop until I hit bottom." There are two reasons why this way of thinking can hurt you:

    First, it's not true. Many chemically dependent people have short-term and low-consequence relapses and do what is necessary to get back into recovery before serious damage occurs.

    Second, this approach programs you to have a long-term catastrophic relapse episode. If you do start to use alcohol or drugs, a voice will pop into your head saying, "If you take one drink or one dose of a drug you will lose control and not be able to stop until you hit bottom." When this voice starts talking, it is easy for another part of you to say, "Great, now I can keep drinking and drugging and enjoy myself until I hit bottom!"

2. Always keep the truth about relapse in mind: If you start to use alcohol or other drugs, it is a serious and life-threatening problem. You will probably hit a moment of sanity where you can choose to stop drinking and drugging and get help. At these moments, it is important to act immediately. If you wait, the urge to drink and drug will come back and the opportunity will be lost.

3. If you start to use alcohol and drugs and hit a moment of sanity where you want to stop, the most effective things for you to do are:

    A. Tell yourself the truth: "I'm in a relapse. If I don't stop, I'll probably destroy myself and hurt those I love. This moment of sanity will disappear in a few minutes. I must seize this moment and do what is necessary to stop."

    B. Immediately stop using and get out of the situation that is supporting your alcohol and drug use.

    C. When out of the situation, call someone who will treat you with dignity and respect and ask them to help you get back into recovery.

    D. Go somewhere that will support your decision to stop using alcohol and other drugs. This might mean calling a therapist or sponsor, going to a treatment program, or getting to a support group meeting.

© Terence T. Gorski, 2000. *Relapse Prevention Counseling Workbook—Practical Exercises for Managing High-risk Situations*, Herald Publishing House/ Independence Press, 1-800-767-8181 or (816) 521-3015; Website *www.relapse.org*. Training and Consulation available from The CENAPS Corporation, Phone: (352) 596-8000; Fax: (352) 596-8002; Website: *www.cenaps.com*; E-mail: *info@cenaps.com*.

4. **The Relapse Intervention Plan:** In its simplest form, developing a relapse intervention plan consists of asking and processing three questions. A specific written plan is developed in response to each question. These questions are:

(1) What is the therapist supposed to do if the client relapses, stops coming to sessions, or fails to honor their treatment contract?

(2) What is the client going to do to get back into recovery if they start using alcohol or drugs and decide to stop using before they hit bottom?

(3) Who are three significant people who have an investment in the client's recovery and what is each of them supposed to do if relapse occurs?

Go to the next page and complete Exercise 2-1.

© Terence T. Gorski, 2000. *Relapse Prevention Counseling Workbook—Practical Exercises for Managing High-risk Situations*, Herald Publishing House/ Independence Press, 1-800-767-8181 or (816) 521-3015; Website *www.relapse.org*. Training and Consulation available from The CENAPS Corporation, Phone: (352) 596-8000; Fax: (352) 596-8002; Website: *www.cenaps.com*; E-mail: *info@cenaps.com*.

Exercise 2-1: Developing the Relapse Intervention Plan

1. I agree to do the following to get back into recovery if I start using alcohol or other drugs and decide that I want to stop using before destroying my life:

   _____

   _____

   _____

   _____

   _____

   _____

   _____

2. I agree to do the following if I stop attending the activities that I agreed to make part of my recovery program:

   _____

   _____

   _____

   _____

   _____

   _____

   _____

   _____

3. I agree to do the following if I want to drop out of treatment against the recommendation of my therapist:

   _____

   _____

   _____

   _____

   _____

   _____

   _____

© Terence T. Gorski, 2000. *Relapse Prevention Counseling Workbook—Practical Exercises for Managing High-risk Situations*, Herald Publishing House/ Independence Press, 1-800-767-8181 or (816) 521-3015; Website *www.relapse.org*. Training and Consulation available from The CENAPS Corporation, Phone: (352) 596-8000; Fax: (352) 596-8002; Website: *www.cenaps.com*; E-mail: *info@cenaps.com*.

4. What do you want your therapist to do if you start using alcohol or other drugs and you tell your therapist about it and ask for help?

    _____

    _____

    _____

    _____

    _____

5. What do you want your therapist to do if you start using alcohol or other drugs and either don't tell your therapist about it or you don't follow through with what you agreed to do to stop the relapse quickly and get back into recovery?

    _____

    _____

    _____

    _____

    _____

6. What do you want your therapist to do if you stop coming to treatment?

    _____

    _____

    _____

    _____

    _____

7. What do you want your therapist to do if you don't complete your recovery assignments?

    _____

    _____

    _____

    _____

    _____

> If you are working with a sponsor, complete questions
> 8 to 10 and discuss them with
> both your therapist and your sponsor.

8. What do you want your sponsor to do if you start using alcohol or other drugs, and you tell your sponsor about it, and ask for help?

_____

_____

_____

_____

_____

9. What do you want your sponsor to do if you start using alcohol or other drugs and either don't tell them about it or don't follow through with what you agreed to do to stop the relapse quickly and get back into recovery?

_____

_____

_____

_____

_____

10. What do you want your sponsor to do if you stop going to meetings or working your program?

_____

_____

_____

_____

_____

© Terence T. Gorski, 2000. *Relapse Prevention Counseling Workbook—Practical Exercises for Managing High-risk Situations*, Herald Publishing House/ Independence Press, 1-800-767-8181 or (816) 521-3015; Website *www.relapse.org*. Training and Consulation available from The CENAPS Corporation, Phone: (352) 596-8000; Fax: (352) 596-8002; Website: *www.cenaps.com*; E-mail: *info@cenaps.com*.

> If you are working with a *significant other*,
> (*your spouse or close friend*) complete questions 11 to 14
> and discuss them with
> both your therapist and your significant other.

11. What do you want your *significant other* (a spouse or close friend) to do if you start using alcohol or other drugs, tell him or her about it, and ask for help?

_____

_____

_____

_____

_____

12. What do you want your *significant other* to do if you start using alcohol or other drugs and either don't tell him or her about it or you don't follow through with what you agreed to do to stop the relapse quickly and get back into recovery?

_____

_____

_____

_____

_____

13. What do you want your *significant other* to do if you stop coming to treatment?

_____

_____

_____

_____

_____

14. What do you want your *significant other* to do if you don't complete your recovery assignments?

_____

_____

_____

_____

_____

Go to the next page and complete Exercise 2-2.

© Terence T. Gorski, 2000. *Relapse Prevention Counseling Workbook—Practical Exercises for Managing High-risk Situations*, Herald Publishing House/Independence Press, 1-800-767-8181 or (816) 521-3015; Website *www.relapse.org*. Training and Consulation available from The CENAPS Corporation, Phone: (352) 596-8000; Fax: (352) 596-8002; Website: *www.cenaps.com*; E-mail: *info@cenaps.com*.

Exercise 2-2: Summarizing the Relapse Intervention Plan

Instructions: Review your answers to the questions in Exercise 2-1 and summarize that information by writing the answers to the following three questions. These questions will help you tie together the information about your relapse intervention plan that you identified in the previous exercise. It will also help you keep a balanced focus that involves you, your counselor or therapist, and the significant people in your life. Here are the questions:

1. What am I (the therapist) supposed to do if you (the client) start using alcohol or drugs, stop coming to treatment, or don't complete your treatment assignments?

    _____

    _____

    _____

    _____

2. What are you (the client) going to do to get back into recovery if you start using alcohol or drugs and decide to stop before getting into serious trouble?

    _____

    _____

    _____

    _____

    _____

3. Who are three significant others who have an investment in your (the client's) recovery and what is each of them supposed to do if relapse occurs?

    A. Significant Other #1:_____

    _____

    _____

    B. Significant Other #2:_____

    _____

    _____

    C. Significant Other #3:_____

    _____

    _____

This exercise stops here.

© Terence T. Gorski, 2000. *Relapse Prevention Counseling Workbook—Practical Exercises for Managing High-risk Situations*, Herald Publishing House/ Independence Press, 1-800-767-8181 or (816) 521-3015; Website *www.relapse.org*. Training and Consulation available from The CENAPS Corporation, Phone: (352) 596-8000; Fax: (352) 596-8002; Website: *www.cenaps.com*; E-mail: *info@cenaps.com*.

19

Exercise #3: Identifying High-risk Situations

A high-risk situation is something that happens that makes us want to use alcohol or drugs after making a commitment not to. We don't get into high-risk situations by accident; we set ourselves up to get drawn into these situations. Some people call it *Building Up to Drink and Drug (BUDD)*. Others call it going *SOUR (Setting Ourselves Up to Relapse)*. Once we're in the situation we don't know what to do. We say that it's really not our fault that we're there, that we didn't plan it, that it just happened and there's nothing we can do about it.

Identifying a high-risk situation can be tricky because the same situation can make some-people want to use alcohol or other drugs and have no effects on other people. Sometimes the same high-risk situation can make us want to use alcohol or other drugs at some times but not at others.

To manage high-risk situations we must first know what our high-risk situations are and how we get into them. We can identify the high-risk situations that put us at risk of relapse by completing two steps: (1) reading a list of the common high-risk situations that can cause relapse, (2) identifying the high-risk situations that apply to you, and (3) writing titles and descriptions of your high-risk situations that make them easy for you to remember and recognize when they happen. (*Exercises 3-1* and *3-2* guide you through these three steps).

The list of high-risk situations in *Exercise 3-1* has been developed to help you to recognize the typical types of situation that can lead you from abstinence back into the use of alcohol and other drugs.

Read this list carefully.

After reading each paragraph, pause for a moment and notice what you are thinking and feeling. You can do this by:

(1)   Putting a check mark ☼ next to any high-risk situation you believe you may experience within the near future;

(2)   Putting a question mark (?) next to any high-risk situation that you have difficulty understanding;

(3)   Putting an asterisk (*) next to any high-risk situation that causes strong or intense feelings as you read it.

(4)   Discussing the high-risk situations that you marked with a check mark, question mark, or asterisk with your therapist, sponsor, and significant others. These discussions will help you develop a better understanding of what they represent and what you need to do to effectively manage them without using alcohol or other drugs.

Go to the next page and complete Exercise 3-1.

Exercise 3-1: Reading the High-risk Situation (HRS) List

☐ 1. **Problems Force Us to Stop:** We have a serious problem or crisis related to our alcohol or drug use. We feel an inner conflict. One part of us wants to keep drinking or drugging despite the problem. Another part of us says no and holds us back because to keep using alcohol and drugs would cause serious problems. We convince ourselves that it would be a good idea to stop drinking and drugging until the situation calms down, but we feel deprived. Because we don't believe we can have a good life without drinking or drugging, we leave the door open to change our mind later when things have calmed down.

☐ 2. **We Don't Make the Connection:** We refuse to see the relationship between our drinking and drugging and the problems we're having. We convince ourselves that we have the right to use despite the problems. Nobody has the right to make us stop. We tell ourselves that the real problem isn't our drinking and drugging. Sure we've got some serious problems. That's why we're drinking and drugging—to help us cope with those problems.

☐ 3. **We Deny We're Addicted:** We tell ourselves we're in control of our alcohol and drug use, it doesn't control us. We can stop any time we want to. We're not drinking or drugging now and that proves we're in control. Nobody is going to convince us that we're some kind of slobbering, no-good, out-of-control drunk or druggie.

☐ 4. **We Push Away People Who Can Help:** We prove we're not an alcoholic or drug abuser by telling ourselves that we have friends and people who care about us and they don't mind our drinking and drugging at all. There are other people who don't like us the way we are. It's these people, who aren't really our friends, who want us to stop. If they were our friends, they wouldn't be causing us problems by sticking their noses where they don't belong. If they'd just leave us alone, everything would be fine.

☐ 5. **We Start Romancing the High:** We start remembering how good it was to use alcohol and drugs in the past. We make our memories bigger than life by exaggerating the good times while minimizing or blocking out the pain and the problems. We start to convince ourselves that we always felt good and never had pain or problems when we were drinking or drugging.

☐ 6. **We Awfulize Being Sober:** We start thinking about how hard it is to stay away from alcohol or drugs. We convince ourselves that it is awful, terrible, and unbearable to have to live without alcohol and drugs. Sober living is nothing but pain, problems, and hassles. Without drinking and drugging we can never have the good life.

☐ 7. **We Use Magical Thinking:** We believe that alcohol and drugs can magically fix us. We know that drinking and drugging would make us feel good and solve all of our problems. We convince ourselves that this time we won't abuse it or lose control. We'll use it responsibly. Besides, it will just be this one time. We'll only use for a short period of time until the pressure is off. Then we'll stop again.

☐ 8. **We Recycle Addictive Thinking:** We keep recycling these three thoughts in our head: *"Remember how good it was! Look at how awful it is that I can't! Imagine how good it would be if only I could do it again."* By recycling these thoughts over and over again we turn the thought (Wouldn't it be nice if I could?) into a desire (I want to do it), into an

© Terence T. Gorski, 2000. *Relapse Prevention Counseling Workbook—Practical Exercises for Managing High-risk Situations*, Herald Publishing House/ Independence Press, 1-800-767-8181 or (816) 521-3015; Website *www.relapse.org*. Training and Consulation available from The CENAPS Corporation, Phone: (352) 596-8000; Fax: (352) 596-8002; Website: *www.cenaps.com*; E-mail: *info@cenaps.com*.

urge (I should be able to do it), and eventually into a craving (I need to do it now, I have no other choice).

☐ 9. **We Get into Problem Situations:** We start putting ourselves into situations that create unnecessary pain and problems.

    A. **We Make Problems Worse:** Sometimes we have a legitimate problem and end up doing things that make it worse instead of better. We shoot ourselves in the foot and feel the pain. Then we reload the gun and shoot ourselves in the other foot.

    B. **We Overcommit:** Sometimes we take on more than we can handle and start missing deadlines and letting other people down. Instead of talking openly about the problem, we go underground, put things off, blame others, and try to cover our tracks. When we get caught we get defensive and try to con our way out of it.

    C. **We Get Frustrated:** Sometimes we get frustrated because we want something that we can't have. When this happens we feel deprived because we should be able to have it. We deserve it. We're entitled to it. Others don't have the right to keep us from getting it.

    D. **We Argue and Fight:** Sometimes we want to have a good time, so we visit our friends, other family members, or our parents. We end up getting into arguments, fights, or conflicts. We leave believing that no one really cares about us or understands us.

    E. **We Want to Fit In:** We feel left out. It seems like no one likes us or wants to be around us. We want to fit in and feel like a normal person, but somehow we just can't see ourselves doing it without alcohol or drugs

☐ 10. **We Get Around Booze or Drugs:** We start putting ourselves in situations where we're around people, places, and things that make us want to drink and drug despite our commitment not to.

    A. **We Want to Feel Better:** We might get into situations where we're feeling good but we want to feel better or enjoy ourselves more.

    B. **We Want to Change Our Energy:** We might get into situations that stress us out or make us feel tired and bored. These situations leave us feeling like we need something to either calm us down or pick us up.

    C. **We Hang Out with Old Friends:** We might accidentally run into old friends we used to drink or use drugs with. We might get invited out by friends or family members, and feel that we can't say no. We don't want to drink or drug, but what's wrong with seeing how they are doing?

    D. **People Start Drinking or Drugging Around Us:** We might be in a social situation and the people we are with start drinking or drugging and offer us some. We suddenly notice that everyone else is using alcohol or drugs. We don't want to drink or drug, but everyone else is and we feel pressured. We remember how good it felt and ask ourselves "Why not?" Besides no one will know.

 © Terence T. Gorski, 2000. *Relapse Prevention Counseling Workbook—Practical Exercises for Managing High-risk Situations*, Herald Publishing House/ Independence Press, 1-800-767-8181 or (816) 521-3015; Website *www.relapse.org*. Training and Consulation available from The CENAPS Corporation, Phone: (352) 596-8000; Fax: (352) 596-8002; Website: *www.cenaps.com*; E-mail: *info@cenaps.com*.

E   **We Want Better Sex:** We might get into a sexual experience that we feel could be enhanced by using alcohol or drugs. Or that sexual experience might not be going as well as we would like. We know that a little alcohol or drugs could reduce our inhibitions, free us up, increase our pleasure, get rid of our shame or guilt, and help to seduce or please our partner.

F.   **We Face a Loss:** A family member or friend might die. We have to go to the funeral and attend the social functions that surround it. We see people drinking. Some are high on drugs and we know it. One relative is walking around offering tranquilizers to anyone who wants them. Then we go home, alone, to deal with the pain and loss. We want to feel better, but we don't know what to do.

G.   **We Remember Bad Experiences:** We might get into situations that remind us of a painful past situation such as the death of a family member, loved one, or friend. Sometimes the situation makes us think of a major failure or loss or some personal trauma or tragedy. We hurt and don't know how to deal with the pain.

H.   **We Feel Trapped:** We might get backed into a corner and start feeling trapped because we don't know what to do. We might get into a situation where we feel isolated or cut off from others. It seems like there is no way to fit in or get connected. To avoid situations like this, we might start spending more time alone and when we're by ourselves we might start to feel lonely.

I.   **We Get Sick:** We might get sick, injured, or start having physical pain or discomfort. Our doctor might offer us a prescription for pain medication, muscle relaxants, or tranquilizers. What's wrong with that? He's a doctor and I'm sick and in pain.

This high-risk situation list was developed with the help of Roland Williams, Arthur B. Trundy, Tim Dworniczek, and Joseph E. Troiani. This high-risk situation list is based, in part, on the research of G. Alan Marlatt and Helen Annis.

Go to the next page and complete Exercise 3-2.

© Terence T. Gorski, 2000. *Relapse Prevention Counseling Workbook—Practical Exercises for Managing High-risk Situations*, Herald Publishing House/ Independence Press, 1-800-767-8181 or (816) 521-3015; Website *www.relapse.org*. Training and Consulation available from The CENAPS Corporation, Phone: (352) 596-8000; Fax: (352) 596-8002; Website: *www.cenaps.com*; E-mail: *info@cenaps.com*.

Exercise 3-2: Identifying and Personalizing Your High-risk Situations

1. **Ask Yourself What Your High-risk Situations Are:** After reading the High-risk Situation List, most of us can identify at least one high-risk situation that can make us want to use alcohol or other drugs despite our commitment not to. Think ahead over the next six weeks and identify the situation that will put you at the greatest risk of using alcohol or other drugs. Write a short sentence that describes this situation.

   _____

   _____

2. **How Does This Situation Increase Your Risk of Using Alcohol or Drugs:** Write a sentence or short paragraph that describes how this situation will make you want to use alcohol or drugs despite your commitment not to.

   _____

   _____

   _____

3. **Write a Personal Title:** A personal title is a word or short phrase that clearly identifies the high-risk situation without having to use a lot of words. On the line below, write a personal title for this high-risk situation.

   Example #1: *Hanging Out with Drinkers at Weddings:*

   Example #2: *Staying Home Alone:*

   _____

4. **Write a Personal Description:** A personal description is a single sentence with a beginning, a middle, and an end that describes the high-risk situation. You can use this format: I know that I am in a high-risk situation when <I do something> that causes <pain or problems> and I want to use alcohol or drugs to manage the pain or to solve the problems. The following examples match the examples of titles given in question 3.

   Example #1: *"I know that I'm in a high-risk situation when I go to a wedding, hang out with relatives I used to drink with, feel left out, and I want to use alcohol and drugs to fit in."*

   Example #2: *"I know that I'm in a high-risk situation when I decide to stay home instead of going to a self-help meeting, get lonely and depressed, and start to feel like drinking to feel better. "*

   On the lines below write a personal description of the high-risk situation that relates to the title you selected in question 3.

   I know that I'm in a high-risk situation when...

   _____

   _____

   _____

   _____

© Terence T. Gorski, 2000. *Relapse Prevention Counseling Workbook—Practical Exercises for Managing High-risk Situations*, Herald Publishing House/ Independence Press, 1-800-767-8181 or (816) 521-3015; Website *www.relapse.org*. Training and Consulation available from The CENAPS Corporation, Phone: (352) 596-8000; Fax: (352) 596-8002; Website: *www.cenaps.com*; E-mail: *info@cenaps.com*.

5. **Belief in Your Ability to Manage the Situation without Alcohol or Drugs:** How strongly do you believe you will be able to manage this situation without using alcohol or drugs?

(Circle the number of your choice below)

0 = I definitely will not use A/D; 5 = 50/50 chance of using A/D; 10 = I definitely will use A/D

0 ----- 1 ----- 2 ----- 3 ----- 4 ----- 5 ----- 6 ----- 7 ----- 8 ----- 9 ----- 10

Why do you rate it this way? _____

_____

_____

_____

_____

6. **Belief in Your Ability to Avoid the Situation:** How strongly do you believe you will be able to avoid getting into this situation?

(Circle the number of your choice below)

0 = I definitely will not use A/D; 5 = 50/50 chance of using A/D; 10 = I definitely will use A/D

0 ----- 1 ----- 2 ----- 3 ----- 4 ----- 5 ----- 6 ----- 7 ----- 8 ----- 9 ----- 10

Why do you rate it that way?_____

_____

_____

_____

_____

This exercise stops here.

© Terence T. Gorski, 2000. *Relapse Prevention Counseling Workbook—Practical Exercises for Managing High-risk Situations*, Herald Publishing House/ Independence Press, 1-800-767-8181 or (816) 521-3015; Website *www.relapse.org*. Training and Consulation available from The CENAPS Corporation, Phone: (352) 596-8000; Fax: (352) 596-8002; Website: *www.cenaps.com*; E-mail: *info@cenaps.com*.

Exercise #4: Mapping and Managing High-risk Situations

This exercise will teach you how to map and manage high-risk situations that you will be facing in the near future. A situation map is a description of exactly *what you do* and *how other people react to what you do* that makes you want to use alcohol or other drugs despite your commitment not to use.

A good situation map describes exactly what you and other people do in a way that lets you clearly see it happening in your mind. When developing a situation map it is helpful to go visual and see the situation in your own mind as if it were the scene of a movie.

Try to see exactly what you or other people are saying and doing in the situation. It is important to put everything that happened into the correct order or sequence. You can do this by thinking about the beginning of the situation and then thinking about the next thing that happened until you reach the end of the situation.

Once you map out the situation it is easy to look for *gaps in the action* by asking yourself: "Where in the action sequence is something missing?" Try to notice where you jump from one thing to the next without a logical transition step and then try to fill in the missing step.

Here are some guidelines that will help you develop situation maps that will give you the most help in learning to manage high-risk situations:

1.   **Imagine that You're Telling a Story:** Describe the exact sequence of events that occurred in the situation as if it were a story with a beginning, a middle, and an end.

2.   **Go Visual and See It Happening in Your Mind:** Go visual and try to see the events in your mind as if they were occurring now. Try to remember the specific things that you saw, heard, felt, and did. Vague or general reports won't be very helpful. It is important to be as concrete and specific as possible.

3.   **Write Down What You See Happening in Your Mind:** Write down the sequence of events you are seeing in your mind.

   A.   Start by asking yourself the question: "When did this high-risk situation begin?"

   B.   Then ask yourself the following questions: (2) Who were you with? (3) What were they doing? (4) What were you doing? (5) What was going on around you? (6) Where did this happen? (7) When did this happen?

   C.   Then start at the beginning of the situation and keep asking yourself the question "What is the next thing that happened?" until you get to the end of the situation. Answer each question by being as concrete and specific as possible. Remember, a situation map will be most helpful when it helps you to see or visualize each step of the situation in your own mind.

   D.   Look for gaps in the action. A gap in the action is a hole in the story. It is something in the situation that you missed or failed to notice. *Sometimes the most important things that we need to know to avoid relapsing in the future are hidden in these gaps in the action.* Once you find a gap in the action, take time to meditate or reflect on the situation and see if you can remember or imagine what happened.

   E.   The next step is to identify three intervention points where you could do something different that would keep you from using alcohol or other drugs and produce a better outcome to the situation.

© Terence T. Gorski, 2000. *Relapse Prevention Counseling Workbook—Practical Exercises for Managing High-risk Situations*, Herald Publishing House/ Independence Press, 1-800-767-8181 or (816) 521-3015; Website *www.relapse.org*. Training and Consulation available from The CENAPS Corporation, Phone: (352) 596-8000; Fax: (352) 596-8002; Website: *www.cenaps.com*; E-mail: *info@cenaps.com*.

Situation mapping can be used in clarifying any problem or situation. In this workbook we will use the situation-mapping process to describe three different situations:

(1)   A past high-risk situation that ended in alcohol and drug use. Because this situation ended in the use of alcohol or other drugs, it must have been managed in a self-defeating way that left no alternative except to use alcohol or other drugs. By mapping out these situations you can see the automatic and unconscious habits that you tend to use with difficult situations. You can also discover the ways that you use to convince yourself that you have no other choice but to use alcohol or drugs. This process will help you see the kinds of thoughts, feelings, and behaviors that set you up to relapse.

(2)   A past high-risk situation that ended without using alcohol or drugs. Because this situation ended without using alcohol or other drugs, you must have done something right. In other words, you managed this situation by using strategies that did not require the use of alcohol and drugs. You can use the situation maps of these successfully managed high-risk situations to *catch yourself doing something right*. This will allow you to identify new and more effective ways of coping with similar future high-risk situations.

(3)   An immediate future high-risk situation that you are facing. Because this situation has not occurred, you will use a technique called mental rehearsal to test out different things you could do to manage the situation. When you use mental rehearsal you think about or imagine what the situation will probably be like and then you think about or imagine different ways of handling the situation in your mind. First you *map out the situation using your old self-defeating ways of handling the situation* that caused you to use alcohol or others drugs in the past. Doing this will help you see exactly what you thought and did that caused you to mismanage the situation.

Go to the next page and complete Exercise 4-1.

© Terence T. Gorski, 2000. *Relapse Prevention Counseling Workbook—Practical Exercises for Managing High-risk Situations*, Herald Publishing House/ Independence Press, 1-800-767-8181 or (816) 521-3015; Website *www.relapse.org*. Training and Consulation available from The CENAPS Corporation, Phone: (352) 596-8000; Fax: (352) 596-8002; Website: *www.cenaps.com*; E-mail: *info@cenaps.com*.

Exercise 4-1: Mapping a High-risk Situation that Ended in A/D Use

1. **Reviewing Your High-risk Situation:** Go back to *Exercise 3-2: Identifying and Personalizing Your High-risk Situation* on page 24 and write the title and description of the high-risk situation that you will be facing in the near future in the spaces below:

    Title of the High-risk Situation: _____

    Description of the High-risk Situation: *I know that I'm in a high-risk situation when*

    _____

    _____

    _____

    _____

2. **Mapping a Situation that Ended in Alcohol or Drug Use:** Think of a specific time in the past when you experienced a high-risk situation that was similar to this and *managed it in a way that caused you to use alcohol or other drugs*. Describe that situation as if it were a story with a beginning, a middle, and an end. Start with the phrase: "The high-risk situation started when..." Continue to build the story step-by-step by asking "What is next thing that happened?" Keep asking that question until you get to the end of the story. You can end the story with a final statement that starts with the words: "What finally happened was... "

    The high-risk situation started when... _____

    _____

    _____

    _____

    _____

    _____

    _____

    _____

    _____

    _____

    _____

    _____

    _____

    _____

    _____

    _____

    _____

    _____

Go to the next page and answer questions about this situation.

---

3. **Identifying What You Wanted:** What did you want to accomplish by managing this situation this way?

_____

_____

_____

4. **Identifying What You Actually Got:** Did you get what you wanted by managing the situation this way?

   ❑ Yes   ❑ No   ❑ Unsure

   Explain:

   _____

   _____

5. **Avoiding the Situation:** What could you have done to responsibly avoid getting into this situation?

   • If you avoided this situation, how would it have changed the outcome?

   _____

   _____

6. **Intervention Point #1:** What could you have done differently near the beginning of the situation to produce a better outcome? (How could you have thought differently? managed your feelings and emotions differently? fought your self-destructive urges differently? acted or behaved differently? reacted differently to other people?)

   _____

   _____

   _____

   • If you do these things, how will it change the outcome?

   _____

   _____

7. **Intervention Point #2:** What could you have done differently near the middle of the situation to produce a better outcome? (How could you have thought differently? managed your feelings and emotions differently? fought your self-destructive urges differently? acted or behaved differently? reacted differently to other people?)

   _____

   _____

   _____

© Terence T. Gorski, 2000. *Relapse Prevention Counseling Workbook—Practical Exercises for Managing High-risk Situations*, Herald Publishing House/ Independence Press, 1-800-767-8181 or (816) 521-3015; Website *www.relapse.org*. Training and Consulation available from The CENAPS Corporation, Phone: (352) 596-8000; Fax: (352) 596-8002; Website: *www.cenaps.com*; E-mail: *info@cenaps.com*.   **29**

- If you do these things, how will it change the outcome?

_____

_____

8. **Intervention Point #3:** What can you do differently near the end of the situation to produce a better outcome? (How could you have thought differently? managed your feelings and emotions differently? fought your self-destructive urges differently? acted or behaved differently? reacted differently to other people?)

_____

_____

_____

- If you do these things, how will it change the outcome?

_____

_____

9. **Stop Relapse Quickly:** If you start using alcohol or drugs, what can you do to stop?

_____

_____

10. **Most Important Thing Learned:** What is the most important thing you learned by completing this exercise?

_____

_____

_____

_____

_____

Go to the next page and map out
a high-risk situation that ended without alcohol or drug use.

 © Terence T. Gorski, 2000. *Relapse Prevention Counseling Workbook—Practical Exercises for Managing High-risk Situations*, Herald Publishing House/ Independence Press, 1-800-767-8181 or (816) 521-3015; Website *www.relapse.org*. Training and Consulation available from The CENAPS Corporation, Phone: (352) 596-8000; Fax: (352) 596-8002; Website: *www.cenaps.com*; E-mail: *info@cenaps.com*.

Exercise 4-2: Mapping a High-risk Situation that Ended without A/D Use

1. **Reviewing Your High-risk Situation:** Before completing this part of the exercise, go back to *Exercise 3-2: Identifying and Personalizing Your High-risk Situation* on page 24 and review the title and description of the high-risk situation that you will be facing in the near future.

2. **Reviewing a Situation that Ended without Alcohol or Drug Use:** Think of a specific time in the past when you experienced a high-risk situation that was similar to the immediate high-risk situation you will be facing and *managed it without using alcohol or other drugs.* Tell the experience as if it were a story with a beginning, a middle, and an end. Start with the phrase: "The high-risk situation started when..." Continue to build the story step-by-step by asking "What is next thing that happened?" Keep asking that question until you get to the end of the story. You can end the story with a final statement that starts with the words: "What finally happened was..."

    The high-risk situation started when...

    _____

    _____

    _____

    _____

    _____

    _____

    _____

    _____

    _____

    _____

    _____

    _____

    _____

    _____

    _____

    _____

    _____

    _____

    _____

    _____

Go to the next page and answer the questions about this situation.

© Terence T. Gorski, 2000. *Relapse Prevention Counseling Workbook—Practical Exercises for Managing High-risk Situations*, Herald Publishing House/ Independence Press, 1-800-767-8181 or (816) 521-3015; Website *www.relapse.org.* Training and Consulation available from The CENAPS Corporation, Phone: (352) 596-8000; Fax: (352) 596-8002; Website: *www.cenaps.com*; E-mail: *info@cenaps.com*.

3. What did you do that allowed you to manage this situation without having to use alcohol or other drugs?

_____

_____

_____

4. Did you get what you wanted by managing the situation this way?

❑ Yes ❑ No ❑ Unsure

Explain:

_____

_____

_____

_____

5. **Intervention Point #1:** What did you do differently near the *beginning* of the situation that helped you manage it without having to use alcohol or other drugs? (How did you think differently? manage your feelings and emotions differently? deal with your self-destructive urges differently? act or behave differently? react differently to other people?)

_____

_____

_____

• When you did these things, how did it change the outcome?

_____

_____

6. **Intervention Point #2:** What did you do differently near the *middle* of the situation that helped you manage it without having to use alcohol or other drugs? (How did you think differently? manage your feelings and emotions differently? deal with your self-destructive urges differently? act or behave differently? react differently to other people?)

_____

_____

_____

• When you did these things, how did it change the outcome?

_____

_____

 © Terence T. Gorski, 2000. *Relapse Prevention Counseling Workbook—Practical Exercises for Managing High-risk Situations*, Herald Publishing House/ Independence Press, 1-800-767-8181 or (816) 521-3015; Website *www.relapse.org*. Training and Consulation available from The CENAPS Corporation, Phone: (352) 596-8000; Fax: (352) 596-8002; Website: *www.cenaps.com*; E-mail: *info@cenaps.com*.

7. **Intervention Point #3:** What did you do differently near the end of the situation that helped you manage it without having to use alcohol or other drugs? (How did you think differently? manage your feelings and emotions differently? deal with your self-destructive urges differently? act or behave differently? react differently to other people?)

_____

_____

_____

• When you did these things, how did it change the outcome?

_____

_____

8. **Most Important Thing Learned:** What is the most important thing you learned by completing this exercise?

_____

_____

_____

_____

_____

> **Go to the next page and map out**
> **a high-risk situation that you will experience in the near future.**

Exercise 4-3: Mapping and Managing a Future High-risk Situation

1. **Reviewing Your High-risk Situation:** Before completing this part of the exercise, go back to *Exercise 3-2: Identifying and Personalizing Your High-risk Situation* on page 24 and in the spaces below write the title and the description of the high-risk situation that you will be facing in the near future:

2. **Mapping Your Future High-risk Situation:** Think of a specific time in the near future when you are likely to experience this high-risk situation. Imagine yourself going through this experience and using your old self-defeating ways of managing the situation that would cause you to use alcohol or other drugs. Tell this imagined experience as if it were a story with a beginning, a middle, and an end. Start with the phrase: "The high-risk situation will start when..." Continue to build the story step-by-step by asking "What is the next thing that will happen?" Keep asking this question until you get to the end of the story. You can end the story with a final statement that starts with the words: "What finally will happen is..." Be sure to imagine how you convince yourself that you have no choice but to use alcohol or other drugs to manage this situation.

The high-risk situation will start when...

_____

_____

_____

_____

_____

_____

Go to the next page and answer the questions about this situation.

34 © Terence T. Gorski, 2000. *Relapse Prevention Counseling Workbook—Practical Exercises for Managing High-risk Situations*, Herald Publishing House/ Independence Press, 1-800-767-8181 or (816) 521-3015; Website *www.relapse.org*. Training and Consulation available from The CENAPS Corporation, Phone: (352) 596-8000; Fax: (352) 596-8002; Website: *www.cenaps.com*; E-mail: *info@cenaps.com*.

3. What did you want to accomplish by managing this situation by using your old self-defeating behaviors and coping strategies?

_____

_____

4. Could you imagine yourself getting what you wanted by using your old self-defeating behaviors and coping strategies?

❑ Yes   ❑ No   ❑ Unsure

Explain:

_____

_____

5. **Avoiding the Situation:** Can you imagine doing something that will allow you to responsibly avoid getting into situations like this?

_____

_____

- If you can avoid this type of situation, how will it change the situation?

_____

_____

6. **Intervention Point #1:** Can you imagine yourself doing something different near the beginning of the situation to produce a better outcome? (How could you have thought differently? managed your feelings and emotions differently? fought your self-destructive urges differently? acted or behaved differently? reacted differently to other people?)

_____

_____

- If you do these things, how will it change the situation?

_____

_____

7. **Intervention Point #2:** Can you imagine yourself doing something different near the middle of the situation to produce a better outcome? (How could you have thought differently? managed your feelings and emotions differently? fought your self-destructive urges differently? acted or behaved differently? reacted differently to other people?)

_____

_____

© Terence T. Gorski, 2000. *Relapse Prevention Counseling Workbook—Practical Exercises for Managing High-risk Situations*, Herald Publishing House/ Independence Press, 1-800-767-8181 or (816) 521-3015; Website *www.relapse.org*. Training and Consulation available from The CENAPS Corporation, Phone: (352) 596-8000; Fax: (352) 596-8002; Website: *www.cenaps.com*; E-mail: *info@cenaps.com*.

- If you do these things, how will it change the situation?

_____

_____

8. **Intervention Point #3:** Can you imagine yourself doing something different near the end of the situation to produce a better outcome? (How could you have thought differently? managed your feelings and emotions differently? fought your self-destructive urges differently? acted or behaved differently? reacted differently to other people?)

_____

_____

_____

- If you do these things, how will it change the outcome?

_____

_____

9. **Stop Relapse Quickly:** If you do relapse as a result of a situation like this, what can you imagine yourself doing to stop the relapse quickly before you experience serious problems?

_____

_____

_____

10. **Most Important Thing Learned:** What is the most important thing you learned by completing this exercise?

_____

_____

_____

_____

_____

This exercise stops here.

 © Terence T. Gorski, 2000. *Relapse Prevention Counseling Workbook—Practical Exercises for Managing High-risk Situations*, Herald Publishing House/ Independence Press, 1-800-767-8181 or (816) 521-3015; Website *www.relapse.org*. Training and Consulation available from The CENAPS Corporation, Phone: (352) 596-8000; Fax: (352) 596-8002; Website: *www.cenaps.com*; E-mail: *info@cenaps.com*.

Exercise #5: Managing Personal Reactions to High-risk Situations

High-risk situations, such as the ones you mapped out in the previous exercise, can activate deeply entrenched habits of thinking, feeling, acting, and relating to others that make us want to use alcohol or other drugs. To effectively manage these high-risk situations, we must learn to understand and control the way we react in these situations. Our chances of managing high-risk situations without using alcohol or drugs goes up as we get better at recognizing and managing our thoughts, feelings, urges, actions, and social reactions that make us want to use alcohol and other drugs.

Let's define some words that will help you understand the process of learning how to manage your reactions to high-risk situations.

Personal Reactions are automatic habitual things we do when something happens. There are four things that we automatically do when something happens to us: we think about it, we have feelings or emotional reactions to it, we get an urge to do something about it, and we actually do something. Each automatic personal reaction can be broken down into its component parts: (1) automatic thoughts, (2) automatic feelings, (3) automatic urges, (4) automatic actions. To learn how to effectively manage high-risk situations, you must learn how to change automatic reactions into conscious choices.

Personal Responses are different from personal reactions. A personal reaction is automatic and unconscious. A response is something we consciously choose to do. A conscious response is a choice. To manage high-risk situations without using alcohol or other drugs we must learn to make better choices about how to respond to the situation. In other words, to change automatic reactions into conscious choices we must choose what we think, how we manage and express our feelings, how we manage our urges, and what we actually do in these situations.

Addictive Thinking is an irrational way of thinking that convinces people that alcohol and drug use is an effective way to manage the pain and problems caused by irresponsible thinking and behavior.

Irresponsible Thinking is an irrational way of thinking about something that causes unnecessary emotional pain and motivates us to do things that will make problems worse.

Addictive Behavior is a way of acting that puts us around people, places, and things that make us want to use alcohol or other drugs.

Irresponsible Behavior is a way of acting out or behaving that causes unnecessary pain and problems.

There are *Emotional Consequences to Thoughts and Actions*. All thoughts and behaviors have logical consequences. Sober and rational thinking allows people to deal with life without experiencing unnecessary emotional pain or the urge to use alcohol or drugs to manage unpleasant feelings. Sober and responsible behavior allows people to conduct their lives and solve their problems without producing unnecessary complications for themselves or others and without having to center their lives around the use of alcohol or other drugs.

Instant Gratification is the desire to feel better now even if it means that you will hurt worse in the future. A person seeking instant gratification wants to do something, anything, that will instantly make them feel better: *They want to feel better now without having to think better or act better first.* This results in a *quick fix mentality*. People seeking instant gratification want to feel good all of the time. They tend to place "feeling good" above all other priorities. This is often based on the mistaken

© Terence T. Gorski, 2000. *Relapse Prevention Counseling Workbook—Practical Exercises for Managing High-risk Situations*, Herald Publishing House/ Independence Press, 1-800-767-8181 or (816) 521-3015; Website *www.relapse.org*. Training and Consulation available from The CENAPS Corporation, Phone: (352) 596-8000; Fax: (352) 596-8002; Website: *www.cenaps.com*; E-mail: *info@cenaps.com*.

belief that *"If I feel better, I will be better and my life will be better!"* They are not interested in living according to a responsible set of principles that will make their lives work well. They want what they want when they want it regardless of the consequences.

Deferred Gratification is the ability to feel uncomfortable or to hurt now in order to gain a benefit or to feel better in the future. People who use deferred gratification *think and act better first in order to feel better later.* To learn how to develop deferred gratification we must get in the habit of *thinking things through before we act them out.* Deferred gratification is based on the belief that there are rules or principles that will make our lives work well in the long run and will give us a firm sense of meaning, purpose, and satisfaction that will allow us to get through the inevitable periods of pain, hard feelings, and frustration that we all experience as a normal part of life and living.

We can learn how to *challenge addictive and irresponsible thoughts.* We must learn how to identify and challenge our addictive and irresponsible thoughts if we want to make responsible choices that will allow us to build an effective and satisfying way of life. The following way of thinking can help you challenge the tendency to seek instant gratification: The healthy goal is to live a good life regardless of how it feels at the moment. Feelings change, effective principles don't. Sober and responsible people live a life based on principles, not feelings. Instant gratification provides what looks like an easy way out. The problem is that this easy way out becomes a trap. Once trapped in a conditioned pattern of instant gratification you will feel cravings when you attempt to break the pattern. But once the pattern is broken, the urges disappear because the long-term beneficial consequences of responsible living kick in.

In this exercise on *managing personal reaction to high-risk situations,* we will learn how to analyze high-risk situations by identifying the thoughts, feelings, urges, actions, and social reactions that make us want to use alcohol or other drugs. Then we will learn how to manage them in a new and more effective way without use of alcohol or other drugs.

The first thing we need to do is to understand how thoughts, feelings, urges, actions, and social reactions relate to one another. Here are some basic principles that can help us understand how this works.

1. *Thoughts cause Feelings.* Whenever we think about something, we automatically react by having a feeling or an emotion.

2. *Thoughts and Feelings work together to cause Urges.* Our way of thinking causes us to feel certain feelings. These feelings, in turn, reinforce the way we are thinking. These thoughts and feelings work together to create an urge to do something. An urge is a desire that may be rational or irrational. The irrational urge to use alcohol or other drugs even though we know it will hurt us is also called craving. It is irrational because we want to use alcohol or other drugs even though we know it will not be good for us.

3. *Urges plus Decisions cause Actions.* A decision is a choice. A choice is a specific way of thinking that causes us to commit to one way of doing things while refusing to do anything else. The space between the urge and the action is always filled with a decision. This decision may be an automatic and unconscious choice that you have learned to make without having to think about it, or this decision can be based on a conscious choice that results from carefully reflecting on the situation and the options available for dealing with it.

4. *Actions cause Reactions from other people.* Our actions affect other people and cause them to react to us. It is helpful to think about our behavior like invitations that we give to

© Terence T. Gorski, 2000. *Relapse Prevention Counseling Workbook—Practical Exercises for Managing High-risk Situations,* Herald Publishing House/ Independence Press, 1-800-767-8181 or (816) 521-3015; Website *www.relapse.org.* Training and Consulation available from The CENAPS Corporation, Phone: (352) 596-8000; Fax: (352) 596-8002; Website: *www.cenaps.com;* E-mail: *info@cenaps.com.*

other people to treat us in certain ways. Some behaviors invite people to be nice to us and to treat us with respect. Other behaviors invite people to argue and fight with us or to put us down. In every social situation we share a part of the responsibility for what happens because we are constantly inviting people to respond to us by the actions we take and how we react to what other people do.

People who relapse usually have one or more of the following problems:

1. *They can't tell the difference between thoughts and feelings.* They tend to believe that they can think anything they want and it won't affect their feelings. Then when they start to feel bad they can't understand why and convince themselves that the only way to feel better is to use alcohol or other drugs.

2. *They can't tell the difference between feelings and urges.* They believe that each feeling carries a specific urge. They don't realize that they can experience a feeling, sit still and breathe into the feeling, and it will go away without being acted out.

3. *They can't tell the difference between urges and actions.* They don't realize that there is a space between urge and action.

4. *They can't control their impulses.* They believe they must do whatever they feel an urge to do. They have never learned that to master impulse control you must learn how to pause, relax, reflect, and decide even when you feel a strong urge to act immediately. Let's look at these four steps of the impulse control process:

   - *Pause* and notice the urge without doing anything about it;

   - *Relax* by taking a deep breath, slowly exhaling, and consciously imagining the stress draining from your body;

   - *Reflect* on what you are experiencing by asking yourself: "What do I have an urge to do? What has happened when I have done similar things in the past? What is likely to happen if I do that now?"; and then

   - *Decide* what you are going to do about the urge. Make a conscious choice instead of acting out in an automatic, unconscious way. When making the choice about what you are going to do, remind yourself that you will be responsible for both the action that you choose to take and its consequences.

   Remember: *Impulse control lives in the space between the urge and the action.*

5. *They can't tell the difference between actions and social reactions.* They tend to believe that people respond to them for no reason at all. They don't link the responses of others to what they do when they are with others. In reality, what we do gives an invitation to other people to treat us in certain ways. Ask yourself: "How do I want to invite other people to treat me in this situation?"

With this in mind, let's complete an exercise that can help you identify and change the thoughts, feelings, urges, actions, and social reactions that can lead you back to using alcohol and other drugs.

**Go to the next page and learn how to handle
the thoughts related to this situation.**

© Terence T. Gorski, 2000. *Relapse Prevention Counseling Workbook—Practical Exercises for Managing High-risk Situations*, Herald Publishing House/ Independence Press, 1-800-767-8181 or (816) 521-3015; Website *www.relapse.org*. Training and Consulation available from The CENAPS Corporation, Phone: (352) 596-8000; Fax: (352) 596-8002; Website: *www.cenaps.com*; E-mail: *info@cenaps.com*.

Exercise 5-1: Managing Thoughts that Cause You to Use

To manage high-risk situations we must learn how to identify the thoughts that can make us want to use alcohol and other drugs. Think of the high-risk situation that you want to learn how to manage without using alcohol and drugs.

1.   Go back to *Exercise 3-2: Identifying and Personalizing Your High-risk Situation* on page 24 and write in the spaces below the title and the description of the high-risk situation that you will be facing in the near future:

Title of the High-risk Situation: _____

Description of the High-risk Situation: *I know that I'm in a high-risk situation when*

_____

_____

_____

2.   Keeping the situation you described above in mind, read each of the thoughts listed below. Ask yourself if you tend to think similar thoughts when you are in this high-risk situation. If you do, put a check mark in the box in front of the thought. Check as many boxes as needed.

❑ 1. I don't have a serious alcohol or drug problem, so there is no good reason for me not to use alcohol or other drugs to deal with this situation.

❑ 2. I have a right to use alcohol or other drugs in this situation and nobody has the right to tell me to stop.

❑ 3. If I use alcohol or other drugs to deal with this situation, nobody will know about it, so what difference will it make?

❑ 4. If I use alcohol or other drugs to deal with this situation, nothing bad will happen to me as a result.

❑ 5. If I don't use alcohol or other drugs, I won't be able to effectively manage this situation.

❑ 6. If I don't use alcohol or other drugs, I won't be able to handle the stress and pain that this situation will cause.

❑ 7. Alcohol or other drugs can help me manage this situation more effectively.

❑ 8. I shouldn't have to do anything special to manage this situation. If I just go with the flow, everything will be OK.

Go on to the next page.

© Terence T. Gorski, 2000. *Relapse Prevention Counseling Workbook—Practical Exercises for Managing High-risk Situations*, Herald Publishing House/ Independence Press, 1-800-767-8181 or (816) 521-3015; Website *www.relapse.org*. Training and Consulation available from The CENAPS Corporation, Phone: (352) 596-8000; Fax: (352) 596-8002; Website: *www.cenaps.com*; E-mail: *info@cenaps.com*.

3. What are three thoughts you tend to have in this kind of high-risk situation that make you want to use alcohol or other drugs? You can use the thoughts above as a starting point, but it is important for you to put these thoughts in your own words.

Thought #1:_____

_____

• What is another way of thinking that could convince you not to use alcohol or other drugs?

_____

_____

Thought #2:_____

_____

• What is another way of thinking that could convince you not to use alcohol or other drugs?

_____

_____

Thought #3:_____

_____

• What is another way of thinking that could convince you not to use alcohol or other drugs?

_____

_____

**Go to the next page and and learn how to handle
the feelings related to this situation.**

© Terence T. Gorski, 2000. *Relapse Prevention Counseling Workbook—Practical Exercises for Managing High-risk Situations*, Herald Publishing House/ Independence Press, 1-800-767-8181 or (816) 521-3015; Website *www.relapse.org*. Training and Consulation available from The CENAPS Corporation, Phone: (352) 596-8000; Fax: (352) 596-8002; Website: *www.cenaps.com*; E-mail: *info@cenaps.com*.

Exercise 5-2: Managing Feelings and Urges that Cause You to Use

The following exercise will show you how to more effectively manage the feeling and emotions that you will tend to experience in your immediate high-risk situation.

1.   Before completing this part of the exercise, go back to Exercise 5-1 on page 40 and read the title and the description of the high-risk situation that you are learning how to manage.

2.   When you are in this high-risk situation do you tend to feel...

☐ *Strong* or ☐ *Weak*? How intense is the feeling? (0–10) _____

Why do you rate it this way? _____

3.   When you are in this high-risk situation do you tend to feel...

☐ *Angry* or ☐ *Caring*? How intense is the feeling? (0–10)_____

Why do you rate it this way? _____

4.   When you are in this high-risk situation do you tend to feel...

☐ *Happy* or ☐ *Sad*? How intense is the feeling? (0–10) _____

Why do you rate it this way? _____

5.   When you are in this high-risk situation do you tend to feel...

☐ *Safe* or ☐ *Threatened*? How intense is the feeling? (0–10)_____

Why do you rate it this way? _____

6.   When you are in this high-risk situation do you tend to feel...

☐ *Fulfilled* or ☐ *Frustrated*? How intense is the feeling? (0–10)_____

Why do you rate it this way? _____

7.   When you are in this high-risk situation do you tend to feel...

☐ *Proud* or ☐ *Ashamed*? How intense is the feeling? (0–10) _____

Why do you rate it this way? _____

8.   When you are in this high-risk situation do you tend to feel...

☐ *Lonely* or ☐ *Connected*? How intense is the feeling? (0–10) _____

Why do you rate it this way? _____

9.   What are the three strongest feelings you tend to have in this kind of high-risk situation that makes you want to use alcohol or other drugs?

Feeling #1: _____

• Why did you choose this feeling?_____

Feeling #2: _____

• Why did you choose this feeling?_____

Feeling #3: _____

• Why did you choose this feeling?_____

© Terence T. Gorski, 2000. *Relapse Prevention Counseling Workbook—Practical Exercises for Managing High-risk Situations*, Herald Publishing House/ Independence Press, 1-800-767-8181 or (816) 521-3015; Website *www.relapse.org*. Training and Consulation available from The CENAPS Corporation, Phone: (352) 596-8000; Fax: (352) 596-8002; Website: *www.cenaps.com*; E-mail: *info@cenaps.com*.

10. Keeping these three feelings in mind, read each of the following statements about your ability to manage your feelings and rate how true it is on a scale of 0-10. ("0" means the statement is not at all true. "10" means the statement is totally true.) Place your answer on the line in front of each statement.

____ A. **Skill #1:** I am able to anticipate situations that are likely to provoke strong feelings and emotions.

____ B. **Skill #2:** I am able to recognize when I am starting to have a strong feeling or emotion.

____ C. **Skill #3:** I am able to stop myself from automatically reacting to the feeling without thinking it through.

____ D. **Skill #4:** I am able to call a time-out in emotionally charged situations before my feelings become unmanageable.

____ E. **Skill #5:** I am able to use an immediate relaxation technique to bring down the intensity of the feeling.

____ F. **Skill #6:** I am able to take a deep breath and notice what I'm feeling.

____ G. **Skill #7:** I am able to find words that describe what I'm feeling and use the feeling list when necessary.

____ H. **Skill #8:** I am able to rate the intensity of my feelings using a ten-point scale.

____ I. **Skill #9:** I am able to consciously acknowledge the feeling and its intensity by saying to myself, "Right now I'm feeling _____ and it's okay to be feeling this way."

____ J. **Skill #10:** I am able to identify what I'm thinking that's making me feel this way and ask myself, "How can I change my thinking in a way that will make me feel better?"

____ K. **Skill #11:** I am able to identify what I'm doing that's making me feel this way and ask myself, "How can I change what I'm doing in a way that will make me feel better?"

____ L. **Skill #12:** I am able to recognize and resist urges to create problems, hurt myself, or hurt other people in an attempt to make myself feel better.

____ M. **Skill #13:** I am able to recognize my resistance to doing things that would help me or my situation, and force myself to do those things despite the resistance.

____ N. **Skill #14:** I am able to get outside of myself and recognize and respond to what other people are feeling.

Go to the next page.

© Terence T. Gorski, 2000. *Relapse Prevention Counseling Workbook—Practical Exercises for Managing High-risk Situations*, Herald Publishing House/ Independence Press, 1-800-767-8181 or (816) 521-3015; Website *www.relapse.org*. Training and Consulation available from The CENAPS Corporation, Phone: (352) 596-8000; Fax: (352) 596-8002; Website: *www.cenaps.com*; E-mail: *info@cenaps.com*.

11. **Strongest Feeling:** Review the three feelings you identified in question 9 on page 42. What is the *strongest feeling* you experience in this high-risk situation?

_____

A. What are you *thinking* that makes you feel this way?

_____

_____

B. What is another way of *thinking* that could make you feel different?

_____

_____

_____

C. What are you *doing* that makes you feel this way?

_____

_____

D. What is another way of *acting* that could make you feel different?

_____

_____

_____

12. **Second Strongest Feeling:** Review the three feelings you identified in question 9 on page 42. What is the *second strongest feeling* you experience in this high-risk situation?

_____

A. What are you *thinking* that makes you feel this way?

_____

_____

B. What is another way of *thinking* that could make you feel different?

_____

_____

_____

C. What are you *doing* that makes you feel this way?

_____

_____

D. What is another way of *acting* that could make you feel different?

_____

_____

_____

13. **Third Strongest Feeling:** Review the three feelings you identified in question 9 on page 42. What is the *third strongest feeling* that you experience in this high-risk situation?

_____

A. What are you *thinking* that makes you feel this way

_____

_____

B. What is another way of *thinking* that could make you feel different?

_____

_____

_____

C. What are you *doing* that makes you feel this way?

_____

_____

D. What is another way of *acting* that could make you feel different?

_____

_____

_____

**Go to the next page and learn how to handle
the urges related to this problem.**

© Terence T. Gorski, 2000. *Relapse Prevention Counseling Workbook—Practical Exercises for Managing High-risk Situations,* Herald Publishing House/ Independence Press, 1-800-767-8181 or (816) 521-3015; Website *www.relapse.org.* Training and Consulation available from The CENAPS Corporation, Phone: (352) 596-8000; Fax: (352) 596-8002; Website: *www.cenaps.com*; E-mail: *info@cenaps.com.*

Exercise 5-3: Managing the Urges that Cause You to Use

High-risk situations often cause the urge to use alcohol and drugs. When this urge or craving is activated we almost always experience an inner struggle between two parts of ourselves. One part, our addictive self, wants to use alcohol or other drugs. Another part of us, the sober self, wants to manage the situation without using alcohol or other drugs. This exercise will help you explore these two parts of yourself.

1. Before completing this part of the exercise, go back to *Exercise 5-1* on page 40 and read the title and description of the high-risk situation you are learning how to manage.

2. When you are in this high-risk situation, what do you have an urge to do?

    _____

    _____

    _____

    _____

3. Is there a part of you that wants to use alcohol and drugs? Tell me about that part.

    _____

    _____

    _____

4. Is there another part of you that wants to manage the situation without using alcohol or drugs? Tell me about that part.

    _____

    _____

    _____

5. If you wanted to manage this high-risk situation more effectively, what part of you do you need to listen to and why?

    _____

    _____

    _____

    _____

**Go to the next page and learn how to handle
the actions related to this situation.**

© Terence T. Gorski, 2000. *Relapse Prevention Counseling Workbook—Practical Exercises for Managing High-risk Situations*, Herald Publishing House/ Independence Press, 1-800-767-8181 or (816) 521-3015; Website *www.relapse.org*. Training and Consulation available from The CENAPS Corporation, Phone: (352) 596-8000; Fax: (352) 596-8002; Website: *www.cenaps.com*; E-mail: *info@cenaps.com*.

Exercise 5-4: Managing the Actions that Cause You to Use

1. Before completing this part of the exercise, go back to Exercise 5-1 on page 40 and read the title and the description of the high-risk situation you are learning how to manage.

2. Keeping this high-risk situation in mind, read the following list of *Self-defeating Behaviors* that can be used to mismanage this high-risk situation. Check the behaviors that you are most likely to use in this situation.

   ❑ 1. *Procrastinating:* I put off dealing with the high-risk situation by finding excuses or reasons for not doing it now.

   ❑ 2. *Distracting Myself:* I get too busy with other things to pay attention to managing the situation.

   ❑ 3. *Saying "It's Not That Important":* I convince myself that other things are more important than effectively managing this high-risk situation.

   ❑ 4. *Thinking I'm Cured:* I convince myself that because I'm OK now and don't have an alcohol or drug problem, there is no need to learn how to manage this high-risk situation more effectively.

   ❑ 5. *Playing Dumb:* Even though a big part of me knows what I need to do to manage this situation more effectively, I let myself get confused and convince myself that I can't understand what I'm supposed to do.

   ❑ 6. *Getting Overwhelmed:* I feel scared and start to panic. I use my fear as an excuse for not learning how to manage the high-risk situation more effectively.

   ❑ 7. *Playing Helpless:* I pretend to be too weak and helpless to manage the situation more effectively.

   ❑ 8. *Wanting the Quick Fix:* I want a guarantee that I can quickly and easily learn to manage the high-risk situation more effectively or I won't even try.

3. What are the three self-defeating behaviors you tend to have in this kind of high-risk situation that make you want to use alcohol or other drugs? You can use the self-defeating behaviors above as a starting point, but it is important for you to write the descriptions in your own words.

   _____

   A.   Self-defeating Behavior #1:_____

   _____

   _____

   • What is another way of behaving that could stop you from using alcohol or other drugs in this situation?

   _____

   _____

   _____

   _____

© Terence T. Gorski, 2000. *Relapse Prevention Counseling Workbook—Practical Exercises for Managing High-risk Situations*, Herald Publishing House/ Independence Press, 1-800-767-8181 or (816) 521-3015; Website *www.relapse.org*. Training and Consulation available from The CENAPS Corporation, Phone: (352) 596-8000; Fax: (352) 596-8002; Website: *www.cenaps.com*; E-mail: *info@cenaps.com*.

B.   **Self-defeating Behavior #2:**_____

_____

_____

- What is another way of behaving that could stop you from using alcohol or other-drugs in this situation?

_____

_____

_____

C.   **Self-defeating Behavior #3:**_____

- What is another way of behaving that could stop you from using alcohol or other drugs in this situation?

_____

_____

_____

4.   When you use these self-defeating behaviors...

A. How do other people react to you in a way that increases your risk of using alcohol or drugs?

_____

_____

B. How could other people react to you in a way that would help you to stay away from alcohol or drugs?

_____

_____

C. What could you do to invite other people to deal with you in a way that would help you stay away from alcohol or drugs when you get into high-risk situations?

_____

_____

_____

Go to the next page and learn how to tie together everything that you have learned about managing this kind of situation.

© Terence T. Gorski, 2000. *Relapse Prevention Counseling Workbook—Practical Exercises for Managing High-risk Situations*, Herald Publishing House/ Independence Press, 1-800-767-8181 or (816) 521-3015; Website *www.relapse.org*. Training and Consulation available from The CENAPS Corporation, Phone: (352) 596-8000; Fax: (352) 596-8002; Website: *www.cenaps.com*; E-mail: *info@cenaps.com*.

Exercise 5-5: Managing Personal Reactions to High-risk Situations

This exercise will help you tie together everything that you have learned from completing *Exercises 5-1* through *5-4*.

1.   Before completing this part of the exercise, go back to *Exercise 5-1* on page 40 and read the title and description of the high-risk situation that you are learning how to manage. Then review your answers to all of the questions in *Exercises 5-1* through *5-4*. Take time to reflect on what you are really saying in your answers. See if you can sense how the answer to each question is somehow connected to all of your other answers. Then complete the questions in the table below:

2. When you're in this high-risk situation, what do you tend to think?	2-a. What is another way of thinking that will allow you to manage this high-risk situation without using alcohol or other drugs?
3. When you're in this high-risk situation, what do you tend to feel?	3-a. What is another way to manage those feelings that will let you manage this situation without using alcohol or other drugs?
4. When you're in this high-risk situation, what do you have an urge to do?	4-a. What is another way of managing this urge that will allow you to manage this situation without using alcohol or other drugs?

© Terence T. Gorski, 2000. *Relapse Prevention Counseling Workbook—Practical Exercises for Managing High-risk Situations*, Herald Publishing House/ Independence Press, 1-800-767-8181 or (816) 521-3015; Website *www.relapse.org*. Training and Consulation available from The CENAPS Corporation, Phone: (352) 596-8000; Fax: (352) 596-8002; Website: *www.cenaps.com*; E-mail: *info@cenaps.com*.

5. When you're in this high-risk situation, what do you usually do?	5-a. What are some other things that you could do that will allow you to manage this situation without using alcohol or other drugs?
_____ _____ _____ _____ _____	_____ _____ _____ _____ _____
6. When you're in this high-risk situation, how do other people usually react?	6-a How could you invite other people to react to you in a way that will help you manage this situation without using alcohol or other drugs?
_____ _____ _____ _____ _____	_____ _____ _____ _____ _____

7. **Most Important Thing Learned:** What is the most important thing you learned by completing this exercise?

_____

_____

_____

_____

_____

_____

_____

This exercise stops here.

Exercise #6: Developing a Recovery Plan

Having a daily and weekly plan will help you recover and avoid relapse. People who successfully recover tend to do certain basic things. These recovery principles are proven. In AA, there is such a strong belief that they work that many people with solid recovery will say, "If you want what we have, do what we did!" and, "It works if you work it!"

However, not everyone in recovery does exactly the same things. Once you understand yourself and the basic principles of recovery and high-risk situation management, you can build an effective personal program for yourself.

When you first read about how to develop an effective recovery plan, you may tend to get defensive. "I can't do all of those things!" you might say to yourself.

I invite you to think about your recovery as if you were hiking in the Grand Canyon and had to jump across a ravine that's about three feet wide and 100 feet deep. It's better to jump three feet too far than to risk jumping one inch too short. The same is true of recovery. It's better to plan to do a little bit more than you need to do than to risk not doing enough. In AA they say, "Half measures availed us nothing! We stood at the turning point."

The basic recovery planning principles described in the following exercises are actually habits of good, healthy living. Anyone who wants to live a responsible, healthy, and fulfilling life will get into the habit of regularly doing these things. For people in recovery, practicing these principles each day is essential. A regular schedule of activities, designed to match your unique profile of recovery needs and high-risk situations, is necessary to get into recovery, stay in recovery, and avoid relapse.

> **Go to the next page and select the recovery activities
> that will be right for you.**

© Terence T. Gorski, 2000. *Relapse Prevention Counseling Workbook—Practical Exercises for Managing High-risk Situations*, Herald Publishing House/ Independence Press, 1-800-767-8181 or (816) 521-3015; Website *www.relapse.org*. Training and Consulation available from The CENAPS Corporation, Phone: (352) 596-8000; Fax: (352) 596-8002; Website: *www.cenaps.com*; E-mail: *info@cenaps.com*.

Exercise 6-1: Selecting Recovery Activities

Read the list of recovery activities below and identify which activities might be helpful in your recovery, the obstacles you face in doing them on a regular basis, and your willingness to overcome those obstacles.

1. **Professional Counseling:** The success of your recovery will depend on regular attendance at recovery education sessions, group therapy sessions, and individual therapy sessions. The scientific literature on treatment effectiveness clearly shows that the more time you invest in professional counseling and therapy during the first two years of recovery, the more likely you are to stay in recovery.

    A. Do I believe I need to do this?   ❑ Yes ❑ No   ❑ Unsure

    B. The obstacles that might prevent me from doing this are:

    _____

    _____

    C. Possible ways of overcoming these obstacles are:

    _____

    _____

    D. Will I put this on my recovery plan?   ❑ Yes ❑ No ❑ Unsure

2. **Self-help Programs:** There are a number of self-help programs such as Alcoholics Anonymous (AA), Narcotics Anonymous (NA), Rational Recovery, and Women For Sobriety that can support you in your efforts to live a sober and responsible life. These programs all have several things in common: (1) they ask you to abstain from alcohol and drugs and live a responsible life; (2) they encourage you to regularly attend meetings, so you can meet and develop relationships with other people who are living sober and responsible lives; (3) they ask you to meet regularly with an established member of the group (usually called a sponsor) who will help you learn about the organization and help you get through the rough spots; and (4) they promote a program of recovery (often in the form of steps or structured exercises that you work on outside of meetings) that focus on techniques for changing your thinking, emotional management, urge management, and behavior. Scientific research shows that the more committed and actively involved you are in self-help groups during the first two years of recovery, the greater your ability to avoid relapse.

    A. Do I believe I need to do this?   ❑ Yes ❑ No   ❑ Unsure

    B. The obstacles that might prevent me from doing this are:

    _____

    _____

    C. Possible ways of overcoming these obstacles are:

    _____

    _____

    D. Will I put this on my recovery plan?   ❑ Yes ❑ No ❑ Unsure

© Terence T. Gorski, 2000. *Relapse Prevention Counseling Workbook—Practical Exercises for Managing High-risk Situations*, Herald Publishing House/Independence Press, 1-800-767-8181 or (816) 521-3015; Website *www.relapse.org*. Training and Consulation available from The CENAPS Corporation, Phone: (352) 596-8000; Fax: (352) 596-8002; Website: *www.cenaps.com*; E-mail: *info@cenaps.com*.

3. **Proper Diet:** What you eat can affect how you think, feel, and act. Many chemically dependent people find that they feel better if they eat three well-balanced meals a day, use vitamin and amino acid supplements, avoid eating sugar and foods made with white flour, and cut back or stop smoking cigarettes and drinking beverages containing caffeine, such as coffee and colas. Recovering people who don't follow these simple principles of healthy diet and meal planning tend to feel anxious and depressed, have strong and violent mood swings, feel constantly angry and resentful, and periodically experience powerful cravings. They're more likely to relapse. Those who follow a proper diet tend to feel better and have lower relapse rates.

A. Do I believe I need to do this? ☐ Yes ☐ No ☐ Unsure

B. The obstacles that might prevent me from doing this are:

_____

_____

C. Possible ways of overcoming these obstacles are:

_____

_____

D. Will I put this on my recovery plan? ☐ Yes ☐ No ☐ Unsure

4. **Exercise Program:** Doing thirty minutes of aerobic exercise each day will help your brain recover and help you feel better about yourself. Fast walking, jogging, swimming, and aerobic classes are all helpful. It's also helpful to do strength-building exercises (such as weight lifting) and flexibility exercises (such as stretching) in addition to the aerobic exercise.

A. Do I believe I need to do this? ☐ Yes ☐ No ☐ Unsure

B. The obstacles that might prevent me from doing this are:

_____

_____

C. Possible ways of overcoming these obstacles are:

_____

_____

D. Will I put this on my recovery plan? ☐ Yes ☐ No ☐ Unsure

5. **Stress Management Program:** Stress is a major cause of relapse. Recovering people who learn how to manage stress without using self-defeating behaviors tend to stay in recovery. Those who don't, tend to relapse. Stress management involves learning relaxation exercises and taking quiet time on a daily basis to relax. It also involves avoiding long hours of working, and taking time for recreation and relaxation.

A. Do I believe I need to do this? ☐ Yes ☐ No ☐ Unsure

B. The obstacles that might prevent me from doing this are:

_____

_____

C. Possible ways of overcoming these obstacles are:

_____

_____

D. Will I put this on my recovery plan?   ❑ Yes ❑ No ❑ Unsure

6.   **Spiritual Development Program:** Human beings have both a physical self (based on the health of our brains and bodies) and a non-physical self (based on the health of our value systems and spiritual lives). Most recovering people find they need to invest regular time in developing themselves spiritually, in other words, exercising the nonphysical aspects of who they are. Twelve-Step programs such as AA provide an excellent program for spiritual recovery, as do many communities of faith and spiritual programs. At the heart of any spiritual program are three activities: (1) *Fellowship*, when you spend time talking with other people who use similar spiritual methods; (2) *Private Prayer and Meditation*, when you take time alone to pray and meditate and to consciously put yourself in the presence of your higher power or consciously reflect on your spiritual self; and (3) *Group Worship*, when you pray and meditate with other people who share a similar spiritual philosophy.

A. Do I believe I need to do this?   ❑ Yes ❑ No ❑ Unsure

B. The obstacles that might prevent me from doing this are:

_____

_____

C. Possible ways of overcoming these obstacles are:

_____

_____

D. Will I put this on my recovery plan?   ❑ Yes ❑ No ❑ Unsure

7.   **Morning and Evening Inventories:** People who avoid relapse and successfully recover learn how to break free of automatic and unconscious self-defeating responses. They learn to live consciously each day, being aware of and taking responsibility for what they're doing and the consequences of their behavior. To stay consciously aware, they take time each morning to plan their day. This is called *A Morning Planning Inventory*. They also take time each evening to review their progress and problems. This is called *An Evening Review Inventory*. They discuss what they learn about themselves with other people who are involved in their recovery program.

A. Do I believe I need to do this?   ❑ Yes ❑ No ❑ Unsure

B. The obstacles that might prevent me from doing this are:

_____

_____

C. Possible ways of overcoming these obstacles are:

_____

_____

D. Will I put this on my recovery plan?   ❑ Yes ❑ No ❑ Unsure

Exercise 6-2: Scheduling Recovery Activities

Instructions: On the next page is a weekly planner that will allow you to create a schedule of weekly recovery activities. Think of a typical week and enter the recovery activities that you plan to routinely schedule in the correct time slot for each day. A *recovery activity* is a specific thing that you do at a scheduled time on a certain day. If you can't enter the activity onto a daily planner at a specific time, it's not a recovery activity. Most people find it helpful to have more than one scheduled recovery activity for each day.

Go to the next page and build a weekly schedule of recovery activities.

© Terence T. Gorski, 2000. *Relapse Prevention Counseling Workbook—Practical Exercises for Managing High-risk Situations*, Herald Publishing House/ Independence Press, 1-800-767-8181 or (816) 521-3015; Website *www.relapse.org*. Training and Consulation available from The CENAPS Corporation, Phone: (352) 596-8000; Fax: (352) 596-8002; Website: *www.cenaps.com*; E-mail: *info@cenaps.com*.

Worksheet: The Weekly Planner

	Sunday	Monday	Tuesday	Wednesday	Thursday	Friday	Saturday
6:00 AM							
6:30 AM							
7:00 AM							
7:30 AM							
8:00 AM							
8:30 AM							
9:00 AM							
9:30 AM							
10:00 AM							
10:30 AM							
11:00 AM							
11:30 AM							
12:00 Noon							
12:30 PM							
1:00 PM							
1:30 PM							
2:00 PM							
2:30 PM							
3:00 PM							
3:30 PM							
4:00 PM							
4:30 PM							
5:00 PM							
5:30 PM							
6:00 PM							
6:30 PM							
7:00 PM							
7:30 PM							
8:00 PM							
8:30 PM							
9:00 PM							
9:30 PM							
10:00 PM							
10:30 PM							

Exercise 6-3: Testing the Schedule of Recovery Activities

Developed by Terence T. Gorski

© Terence T. Gorski, 1982, 1997

The CENAPS Corporation

Phone: (352) 596-8000

13194 Spring Hill Drive, Spring Hill, FL 34609

Fax: (352) 596-8002

Website: *www.cenaps.com*

E-mail: *info@cenaps.com*

1. Go back to *Exercise 5-5: Managing Personal Reactions to High-risk Situations*. Think about the primary high-risk situations that you want your recovery program to help you identify and manage. What was the personal title and personal description you gave to this high-risk situation? What were the thoughts, feelings, urges, and actions you tended to have when you were in this kind of situation? What new thoughts and behaviors do you need to develop to manage this high-risk situation with using alcohol or other drugs. Take time to reflect on what you are really saying in your answers.

2. Look at your Weekly Planner. What's the *most important* recovery activity that will help you manage this high-risk situation? Write that recovery activity on the following line:

    _____

    A. How can you use this recovery activity to help you identify this high-risk situation should it occur? (Remember, we are often unaware of most high-risk situations until we feel the urge to use alcohol or other drugs. The purpose of the regularly scheduled recovery activities is to build in a time each day to think about our life situations and how well we are managing them.)

        _____

        _____

        _____

    B. If you start to experience this high-risk situation again, how can you use this recovery activity to manage it? (Remember, managing a high-risk situation means changing how you think, feel, and act. How can this recovery activity help you stop thinking and doing things that make you feel like using alcohol or other drugs? How can it help you start thinking and doing things that make you want to stay clean and sober?)

        _____

        _____

        _____

© Terence T. Gorski, 2000. *Relapse Prevention Counseling Workbook—Practical Exercises for Managing High-risk Situations*, Herald Publishing House/Independence Press, 1-800-767-8181 or (816) 521-3015; Website *www.relapse.org*. Training and Consulation available from The CENAPS Corporation, Phone: (352) 596-8000; Fax: (352) 596-8002; Website: *www.cenaps.com*; E-mail: *info@cenaps.com*.

57

3. Look at your Weekly Planner again. What's the *second most important* recovery activity that will help you manage this high-risk situation?

    A. How can you use this recovery activity to help you identify this high-risk situation should it occur?

    _____

    _____

    _____

    _____

    B. If you start to experience this high-risk situation again, how can you use this recovery activity to manage it?

    _____

    _____

    _____

    _____

4. Look at your Weekly Planner one last time. What's the *third most important* recovery activity that will help you manage this high-risk situation?

    A. How can you use this recovery activity to help you identify this high-risk situation should it occur?

    _____

    _____

    _____

    _____

    B. If you start to experience this high-risk situation again, how can you use this recovery activity to manage it?

    _____

    _____

    _____

    _____

5. What other recovery activities can you think of that might be more effective in helping you identify and manage this high-risk situation if it is activated?

    _____

    _____

    _____

    _____

This exercise stops here.

© Terence T. Gorski, 2000. *Relapse Prevention Counseling Workbook—Practical Exercises for Managing High-risk Situations*, Herald Publishing House/ Independence Press, 1-800-767-8181 or (816) 521-3015; Website *www.relapse.org*. Training and Consulation available from The CENAPS Corporation, Phone: (352) 596-8000; Fax: (352) 596-8002; Website: *www.cenaps.com*; E-mail: *info@cenaps.com*.

Exercise 6-4: Using a Daily Plan to Manage High-risk Situations

Instructions: When learning how to manage high-risk situations it is important to recognize the need for conscious daily planning. We often get ourselves into high-risk situations without consciously thinking about it. By using a daily plan, we can train ourselves to stay aware of high-risk situations and to make conscious decisions about how to manage them when they do occur.

The most effective way of working with a daily plan is to do a *Morning Planning Inventory* every morning and an *Evening Review Inventory* every night before bed. The morning planning inventory takes about fifteen minutes. It helps you plan your day, schedule your recovery activities, and stay aware of any warning signs you might experience. The evening review inventory takes about fifteen minutes. It helps you review the activities of your day, evaluate how well you stuck to your recovery program, and notice if you experienced any relapse warning signs. It also gives you a chance to decide if you need help or support in dealing with what happened during the day.

The following forms are recommended for use during your morning and evening inventories. Make copies of these forms and use them every day.

© Terence T. Gorski, 2000. *Relapse Prevention Counseling Workbook—Practical Exercises for Managing High-risk Situations*, Herald Publishing House/ Independence Press, 1-800-767-8181 or (816) 521-3015; Website *www.relapse.org*. Training and Consulation available from The CENAPS Corporation, Phone: (352) 596-8000; Fax: (352) 596-8002; Website: *www.cenaps.com*; E-mail: *info@cenaps.com*.

Using a Morning Planning Inventory Form

Instructions: Each morning, list your major goals for the day. In the first column, enter the recovery tasks you plan to complete today and then enter the other daily tasks you plan to complete. In column 2, assign a specific time when you plan to complete each recovery task and other daily tasks.

Major Goals for Today: Day: _____   Date: _____

☐ 1. _____

☐ 2. _____

☐ 3. _____

☐ 4. _____

☐ 5. _____

Recovery Tasks	Daily Time Plan
☐ 1.	6:00–7:00
☐ 2.	7:00–8:00
☐ 3.	8:00–9:00
☐ 4.	9:00–10:00
☐ 5.	10:00–11:00
Daily Tasks	11:00–12:00
☐ 1.	12:00–1:00
☐ 2.	1:00–2:00
☐ 3.	2:00–3:00
☐ 4.	3:00–4:00
☐ 5.	4:00–5:00
☐ 6.	5:00–6:00
☐ 7.	6:00–7:00
☐ 8.	7:00–8:00
☐ 9.	8:00–9:00
☐ 10.	9:00–10:00
☐ 11.	**Notes**
☐ 12.	
☐ 13.	
☐ 14.	
☐ 15.	

© Terence T. Gorski, 2000. *Relapse Prevention Counseling Workbook—Practical Exercises for Managing High-risk Situations*, Herald Publishing House/ Independence Press, 1-800-767-8181 or (816) 521-3015; Website *www.relapse.org*. Training and Consulation available from The CENAPS Corporation, Phone: (352) 596-8000; Fax: (352) 596-8002; Website: *www.cenaps.com*; E-mail: *info@cenaps.com*.

Exercise 6-5: Using an Evening Review Inventory

Instructions: Each evening before you go to bed, review your morning plan and then answer the questions below.

1. **Personal and Professional Progress**

   Did I make progress today toward the accomplishment of my personal and professional goals?

   ❑ Yes ❑ No ❑ Unsure

   How do I feel about that progress? _____

   _____

2. **Personal and Professional Problems**

   Did I make progress today toward solving my personal and professional problems?

   ❑ Yes ❑ No ❑ Unsure

   How do I feel about those problems? _____

   _____

3. **High-risk Situations**

   Did I experience any high-risk situations? ❑ Yes ❑ No ❑ Unsure

   If yes, briefly describe the situations you experienced: _____

   _____

   _____

   Did I think about or feel like using alcohol or other drugs in any of these situations?

   ❑ Yes ❑ No ❑ Unsure

   What did I do to manage these high-risk situations? _____

   _____

   _____

   How do I feel about these high-risk situations and how I managed them? _____

   _____

   _____

4. **Decision about the Need for Outside Help**

   Do I need to talk to someone about today's events? ❑ Yes ❑ No ❑ Unsure

   Do I need outside help with the high-risk situations I experienced today?

   ❑ Yes ❑ No ❑ Unsure

   What feelings am I experiencing as I think about my need for outside help?

   _____

   _____

Exercise #7: Evaluating High-risk Situation Management Skills

Instructions: The ultimate test of whether you have benefited from this training will be your ability to manage high-risk situations without using alcohol or other drugs. This evaluation will help you identify your areas of strength and weakness so you will be able to improve your overall skill at managing high-risk situations.

Read each statement below and evaluate your level of skill before participating in this training and your current level of skill after participating in this training.

1. What was the primary goal you wanted to achieve by completing this workbook?

    _____

    _____

2. What was your level of goal attainment? ❑ Full   ❑ Partial   ❑ None
    Why did you rate it this way?

    _____

    _____

3. What is the most important thing you learned about yourself by completing this workbook?

    _____

    _____

4. What will you do differently as a result of what you learned?

    _____

    _____

5. The following questions will help you rate your skills at successfully managing high-risk situations.

    Skill #1: ***Making the Commitment to Stop Using:*** I am able to make and maintain a strong commitment to abstain from alcohol and drug use by reviewing the problems that brought me into treatment, clarifying the relationship of those problems to alcohol and drug use, and projecting the logical consequences of continuing to use alcohol and drugs despite those problems.

    - *Level of Commitment to Abstinence:*
      Before: (0–10) _____ *After: (0–10)* _____

    Skill #2: ***Planning to Stop Relapse Quickly if It Occurs:*** I am able to develop a plan to stop relapse quickly should it occur by clearly defining what my counselor will do, what I will do, and what I want significant people in my life to do if I start using alcohol or other drugs.

    - *Strength of My Relapse Intervention Plan:*
      Before: (0–10) _____ *After: (0–10)* _____

Skill #3: *Identifying High-risk Situations:* I am able to identify the high-risk situations that can cause me to use alcohol or drugs despite my commitment not to by reading the high-risk situation list, identifying high-risk situations that I may experience in the near future, and writing personal titles and description for each high-risk situation.

- *My Skill at Identifying High-risk Situations:*
  Before: (0–10) _____ *After: (0–10)* _____

Skill #4: *Mapping and Managing High-risk Situations:* I am able to use Situation Mapping to describe past high-risk situations that ended in alcohol and drug use, past high-risk situations that did not end in alcohol or drug use, and high-risk situations I may experience in the near future.

- *My Skill at Mapping High-risk Situations:*
  Before: (0–10) _____ *After: (0–10)* _____

Skill #5: *Changing Personal Response to High-risk Situations:* I am able to identify and manage the thoughts, feelings, urges, actions, and social reactions that caused me to mismanage high-risk situations in the past.

- *My Skill at Changing My Personal Responses to High-risk Situations:*
  Before: (0–10) _____ *After: (0–10)* _____

Skill #6: *Developing Recovery Plans:* I am able to develop a schedule of recovery activities that will support my ongoing identification and management of high-risk situations and help me intervene early should relapse occur.

- *My Skill at Using Recovery Plans to Manage High-risk Situations:*
  Before: (0–10) _____ *After: (0–10)* _____

Overall Skill at Managing High-risk Situations: How would you rate the changes in your overall ability to manage the high-risk situations that increase your risk of relapse?

- *Skill Level: Before: (0–10)* _____ *After: (0–10)* _____

- *Why did you rate your changes in skill levels this way?*

_____

_____

_____

_____

This exercise stops here.

© Terence T. Gorski, 2000. *Relapse Prevention Counseling Workbook—Practical Exercises for Managing High-risk Situations*, Herald Publishing House/ Independence Press, 1-800-767-8181 or (816) 521-3015; Website *www.relapse.org*. Training and Consulation available from The CENAPS Corporation, Phone: (352) 596-8000; Fax: (352) 596-8002; Website: *www.cenaps.com*; E-mail: *info@cenaps.com*.

A Final Word

Congratulations! You now belong to a growing group of recovering people who have invested the time and energy to learn how to identify and manage high-risk situations.

The clinical exercises you learned by completing this workbook can be used immediately to help you identify and manage the high-risk situations that cause relapse. Hopefully, you will have internalized a system of problem solving that can be applied to many problems that you will experience in your recovery.

Many of you will fully recover using your self-help program, counseling, and the high-risk situation management skills that you learned. For some, however, these skills will not be enough. For some of you, especially those of you who were raised in a dysfunctional family, may need to go beyond the management of high-risk situations and learn how to identify and change the core personality and lifestyle issues that cause relapse. The psychotherapy process that can help you do this is *Relapse Prevention Therapy (RPT)*. You can take this next step in your recovery by learning these RPT Skills through the completion of the workbook titled: *The Relapse Prevention Therapy Workbook: Managing Core Personality and Lifestyle Problems*.

The challenge of recovery is never really over. It seems that once we start a recovery process, we are either growing or we're dying. There is no standing still. We either commit ourselves each day to improving and refining our recovery skills, or we become complacent and slowly move toward meaninglessness, misery, and relapse. We must make a conscious choice each day about which path we'll follow.

As you move from completing the workbook to using your new skills in real life situations, remember that temporary setbacks may occur, but you can always choose to get back into recovery. Recovery is possible. By completing this workbook you have already taken a big step and begun improving your recovery and lowering your risk of relapse. You next job is to use the skills you have learned in your day-to-day life.

Remember, if you get stuck anywhere in the process of identifying and managing high-risk situations, you can go to our website: *www.cenaps.com* and post your questions on our *treatment bulletin board*. Many of our certified relapse prevention specialists routinely check the bulletin board and respond to questions. You can also share your experience and insight with others.

Good luck on your personal journey! I'm pleased and proud to have walked with you for a little while along the way. Thank you for permitting me to do so!

—*Terence T. Gorski*

> Tomorrow Will Be New Again
>
> If We Have the Strength to Reach for Beauty
>
> And the Spirit to Pay Its Price!

© Terence T. Gorski, 2000. *Relapse Prevention Counseling Workbook—Practical Exercises for Managing High-risk Situations*, Herald Publishing House/Independence Press, 1-800-767-8181 or (816) 521-3015; Website *www.relapse.org*. Training and Consulation available from The CENAPS Corporation, Phone: (352) 596-8000; Fax: (352) 596-8002; Website: *www.cenaps.com*; E-mail: *info@cenaps.com*.

Appendix #1: Additional Resources for Relapse Prevention Planning

Terence T. Gorski and the CENAPS Corporation have developed a core technology package for relapse prevention. This package is designed to meet the needs of cost containment while providing effective and high-integrity approaches to treatment. This series maintains the same principles that have made Relapse Prevention Therapy a preferred approach for the chemical dependency field. It simplifies and streamlines the procedures and extends them to the treatment of mental and personality disorders.

The series contains two relapse prevention workbooks: *The Relapse Prevention Counseling Workbook* and *The Relapse Prevention Therapy Workbook*. Both workbooks are targeted, strategic, and effective. Both allow you to identify the critical relapse warning signs that lead from stable recovery to relapse, and to identify and manage the irrational thoughts, unmanageable feelings, self-destructive urges, and self-defeating behaviors that drive these relapse warning signs. You should be aware of some differences between the two workbooks.

The Relapse Prevention Counseling Workbook presents seven powerful clinical processes designed to identify a key or critical warning sign quickly and teach clients to manage the irrational thoughts, unmanageable feelings, and self-destructive urges driving that warning sign. This workbook presents a counseling process that is most appropriate for people in early recovery who have a clearly identified warning sign or high-risk situation. The process can usually be completed in seven to fourteen sessions.

The Relapse Prevention Therapy Workbook presents fifteen core processes that are divided into five sections: stabilization, assessment, warning sign identification, warning sign management, and recovery planning. This workbook presents a psychotherapy process that relates current warning signs to the core dynamics of personality that drive them. As a result, it is most appropriate for clients with a stable recovery who are willing and able to examine childhood patterns and relate those patterns to the problem of relapse. This process is more involved than simple warning sign identification and management and can usually be completed in fifteen to thirty sessions depending on the severity of the problems identified during the process.

In brief, *The Relapse Prevention Counseling Workbook* is a quick and easy way to identify and clarify immediate problems that threaten recovery. *The Relapse Prevention Therapy Workbook* is ideal for people who want to go in-depth by identifying the core personality-driven patterns that repeatedly compel them into the self-defeating behaviors that lead to relapse.

In addition, Terence T. Gorski's Relapse Prevention Core Technology Package offers a variety of materials for clinicians and recovering people. These include:

- *Staying Sober: A Guide for Relapse Prevention*, the world-renowned, easy-to-read book on addiction, recovery, and relapse prevention. (Available in English, Spanish, Polish, Swedish, Danish, Russian, and Bengali.)

- *The Staying Sober Workbook*, the classic companion workbook to *Staying Sober*. (Available in English and Spanish.)

- *How to Start Relapse Prevention Support Groups*, a must for recovering people and therapists who want to strengthen recovery with a time-proven self-help format. (Available in English and Spanish.)

- *The Phases and Warning Signs of Relapse*, a handy pamphlet that provides at-a-glance descriptions that can help stop relapse before it happens. (Available in English and Spanish.)

- The Staying Sober Recovery Education Modules, a comprehensive, ready-to-use, highly adaptable professional education program for recovery and relapse prevention.

- The Addiction, Recovery, and Relapse Videotape Series, a powerful recovery education program. (Also available on DVD.)

These and many other materials are available from Herald Publishing House/Independence Press, P.O. Box 390, Independence, MO 64051-0390, 1-800-767-8181 or at *www.relapse.org*. For information about training and consultation, or to find a Certified Relapse Prevention Specialist in your area, call or write to The CENAPS Corporation, 6193 Deltona Blvd. Spring Hill, FL 34606; telephone: (352) 596-8000; or website: *www.cenaps.com*.

Appendix #2: Treatment Plan for Managing High-risk Situations

Developed by Terence T. Gorski   © Terence T. Gorski, 1982, 1997

The CENAPS Corporation

Website: *www.cenaps.com*   E-mail: *info@cenaps.com*

1. **Problem Title:** High Risk of Relapse

2. **Problem Description:** The client has made a commitment to abstain from alcohol and other drugs for a period of time and is facing a number of immediate high-risk situations that could cause alcohol or drug use despite that commitment.

3. **Goal:** The client will be able to maintain abstinence by identifying and effectively managing the immediate high-risk situations that can cause relapse.

   - **Start Date:** _____ **Target Date:** _____ **Actual Date:** _____

4. **Interventions:** The client will participate in a combination of group and individual therapy sessions, psychoeducational sessions, supervised study halls, and self-help group meetings where the following interventions will be implemented:

   (1) **The Abstinence Contract:** The client will agree to abstain from alcohol and drugs for the duration of treatment and to complete alcohol and drug testing on a random basis or if requested for any reason by the counselor.

      - **Start Date:** _____ **Target Date:** _____ **Actual Date:** _____
      - **Resources:** RPC Workbook: Exercise #1: Making a Commitment to Stop Using
      - **Assisted By:** _____

      Level of Completion: ❏ Full ❏ Partial ❏ None   Completion Score (0–10) _____

      Notes: _____

   (2) Relapse Early Intervention Plan: The client will complete a relapse early intervention plan that describes the responsibilities of the client, therapist, and significant others to stop relapse quickly should it occur.

      - **Start Date:** _____ **Target Date:** _____ **Actual Date:** _____
      - **Resources:** RPC Workbook: Exercise #2: Planning to Stop Relapse Quickly if It Occurs
      - **Assisted By:** _____

      Level of Completion: ❏ Full ❏ Partial ❏ None   Completion Score (0–10) _____

      Notes: _____

   (3) **Identifying High-risk situations:** The client will identify immediate high-risk situations that can cause the use of alcohol and drugs despite their commitment not to, review the high-risk situation list, and write personal titles and personal descriptions for use in self-monitoring.

      - **Start Date:** _____ **Target Date:** _____ **Actual Date:** _____
      - **Resources:** RPC Workbook: Exercise #2: Planning to Stop Relapse Quickly if It Occurs
      - **Assisted By:** _____

      Level of Completion: ❏ Full ❏ Partial ❏ None   Completion Score (0–10) _____

      Notes: _____

© Terence T. Gorski, 2000. *Relapse Prevention Counseling Workbook—Practical Exercises for Managing High-risk Situations*, Herald Publishing House/ Independence Press, 1-800-767-8181 or (816) 521-3015; Website *www.relapse.org.* Training and Consulation available from The CENAPS Corporation, Phone: (352) 596-8000; Fax: (352) 596-8002; Website: *www.cenaps.com*; E-mail: *info@cenaps.com.*

(4) **Mapping and Managing High-risk Situations:** The client will objectively describe past and future high-risk situations that were mismanaged in a way that led to alcohol and drug use and identify new and more effective management strategies:

- **Start Date:** _____ **Target Date:** _____ **Actual Date:** _____

- **Resources:** RPC Workbook: Exercise #4: Mapping and Managing High-risk Situations _

- **Assisted By:** _____

| Level of Completion: ☐ Full ☐ Partial ☐ None   Completion Score (0–10) _____ |

Notes: _____

(5) **Changing Personal Responses to High-risk Situations:** The client will identify the thoughts, feelings, urges, actions, and social reactions related to managing each high-risk situation in a way that leads to alcohol and drug use and identify new and more effective thoughts, feeling and urge management strategies, actions, and social responses.

- **Start Date:** _____ **Target Date:** _____ **Actual Date:** _____

- **Resources:** RPC Workbook: Exercise #5: Managing Personal Reactions to High-risk Situations

- **Assisted By:** _____

| Level of Completion: ☐ Full ☐ Partial ☐ None   Completion Score (0–10) _____ |

Notes: _____

(6) **Developing Recovery Plans:** The client will develop a schedule of recovery activities that supports the ongoing identification and sober management of high-risk situations.

- **Start Date:** _____ **Target Date:** _____ **Actual Date:** _____

- **Resources:** RPC Workbook: Exercise #6: Developing a Recovery Plan

- **Assisted By:** _____

| Level of Completion: ☐ Full ☐ Partial ☐ None   Completion Score (0–10) _____ |

Notes: _____

(7) **Personal Evaluation of High-risk Management Skills:** The client will do a personal evaluation of current skills at managing high-risk situations.

- **Start Date:** _____ **Target Date:** _____ **Actual Date:** _____

- **Resources:** RPC Workbook: Exercise #7: Evaluating High-risk Situation Management Skills

| Level of Completion: ☐ Full ☐ Partial ☐ None   Completion Score (0–10) _____ |

Notes: _____

8. **Overall Response:** The client has developed the overall ability to anticipate, identify, and responsibly manage critical high-risk situations without using alcohol or drugs.

Notes: _____

_____

_____

_____

_____

| Overall Level of Completion: ☐ Full ☐ Partial ☐ None   Completion Score (0–10) _____ |

© Terence T. Gorski, 2000. *Relapse Prevention Counseling Workbook—Practical Exercises for Managing High-risk Situations*, Herald Publishing House/Independence Press, 1-800-767-8181 or (816) 521-3015; Website *www.relapse.org.* Training and Consulation available from The CENAPS Corporation, Phone: (352) 596-8000; Fax: (352) 596-8002; Website: *www.cenaps.com*; E-mail: *info@cenaps.com.*

Appendix #3: The Abstinence Commitment-Group Reporting Form

1. Presenting Problems:	2. Relationship to Alcohol or Drug Use:	3. Consequences of Not Stopping:		
What are the presenting problems that caused you to seek treatment at this time? (Why did you seek treatment now? Why not yesterday or next week? What would have happened if you didn't seek treatment now? What problems or negative consequences can treatment help you avoid?)	How is each presenting problem related to your use of alcohol or drugs? (Did alcohol or drug use cause this problem? [i.e. Would you have this problem if you never used alcohol or drugs?] Did using make it worse than if you hadn't been using? Did you use to deal with stress or pain caused by this problem?)	What will happen to your ability to solve this problem if you don't stop using alcohol and drugs? (What are the benefits of continuing to use? The disadvantages? What is the best thing, the worst thing, and the most likely thing that could happen if you keep using? What other problems could you have if you keep using?)		
Problem #1:		*Best:*		
		Worst:		
		Most Likely:		
Problem #2:		*Best:*		
		Worst:		
		Most Likely:		
Problem #3:		*Best:*		
		Worst:		
		Most Likely:		
Problem #4:		*Best:*		
		Worst:		
		Most Likely:		
Problem #5:		*Best:*		
		Worst:		
		Most Likely:		

© Terence T. Gorski, 2000. *Relapse Prevention Counseling Workbook—Practical Exercises for Managing High-risk Situations*, Herald Publishing House/ Independence Press, 1-800-767-8181 or (816) 521-3015; Website *www.relapse.org*. Training and Consulation available from The CENAPS Corporation, Phone: (352) 596-8000; Fax: (352) 596-8002; Website: *www.cenaps.com*; E-mail: *info@cenaps.com*.

4. **Need to Stop:** Do you believe it is in your best interest to stop using alcohol and drugs?

❑ Yes ❑ No ❑ Unsure Explain your answer:

_____

_____

5. **Obstacles to Stopping:** What things in your life will make it hard to stop using alcohol or other drugs even though you have made the decision to do so?

_____

_____

_____

6. **Commitment to Stop:** Are you willing to make a commitment to abstain from alcohol and other drugs for the duration of treatment and participate in random and on-request alcohol and drug testing?

❑ Yes ❑ No ❑ Unsure Explain your answer:

_____

_____

7. **Obstacles to Staying Stopped:** What *high-risk situations* are you facing in the near future that could tempt you or cause you to start using alcohol or drugs despite your commitment not to?

High-risk Situation #1:_____

_____

High-risk Situation #2:_____

_____

High-risk Situation #3:_____

_____

8. **Making a Commitment to Treatment:** Do you believe you could benefit from treatment designed to help you overcome the obstacles to stopping and staying stopped? Are you willing to accept a referral to a program that can provide that treatment process?

❑ Yes ❑ No ❑ Unsure Explain your answer:

_____

_____

_____

Appendix #4: Relapse Intervention Contract:

1.   The client, _____, agrees to do the following if he or she starts using alcohol or other drugs and then decides to stop using.

_____

_____

_____

_____

_____

_____

_____

_____

2.   The therapist (treatment program), _____, agrees to do the following if the client (named above) starts using alcohol or other drugs, asks for help, and does all of the things that were agreed to in item #1 above.

_____

_____

_____

_____

_____

_____

_____

3.   The therapist (treatment program), _____, agrees to do the following if the client (named above) starts using alcohol or other drugs and does not do the things that were agreed to in item #1 above.

_____

_____

_____

_____

_____

_____

_____

_____

This relapse intervention contract was developed by Arthur B. Trundy.

© Terence T. Gorski, 2000. *Relapse Prevention Counseling Workbook—Practical Exercises for Managing High-risk Situations*, Herald Publishing House/ Independence Press, 1-800-767-8181 or (816) 521-3015; Website *www.relapse.org*. Training and Consulation available from The CENAPS Corporation, Phone: (352) 596-8000; Fax: (352) 596-8002; Website: *www.cenaps.com*; E-mail: *info@cenaps.com*.

Notes

Relapse Prevention Therapy Workbook

Identifying Early Warning Signs Related to Personality and Lifestyle Problems

By Terence T. Gorski and Stephen F. Grinstead

Updated, Revised, and Simplified

The *Relapse Prevention Therapy Workbook* is designed for people in recovery from alcohol or other drug addiction who have a history of relapse, or are currently afraid they might relapse. There continues to be confusion and misunderstanding about what relapse is and how it happens. In this workbook, Terry Gorski and Steve Grinstead clarify their definition of relapse, how it happens, and most importantly how to prevent a person from entering the relapse cycle.

For several years, Gorski and Grinstead have been co-teaching, modifying the process, and field testing all of the exercises contained in this newly revised, simplified, and updated version of the *Relapse Prevention Therapy Workbook*. If a person is willing to be open and honest as well as actively complete each of the 14 developmental exercises in this new workbook, they may never have to experience the pain of relapse again.

ISBN 978-0-8309-1487-6

Herald Publishing House/Independence Press
1-800-767-8181   or   (816) 521-3015

Denial Management Counseling Workbook
Practical Exercises for Motivating Substance Abusers to Recover

By Terence T. Gorski
with Stephen F. Grinstead

Learn to Effectively Manage Denial
In the Treatment of Addiction and Related Personality and Mental Disorders

The *Denial Management Workbook* is designed to help people overcome denial, recognize their addiction, and make a personal commitment to recovery.

Denial is a normal and natural response for coping with painful and overwhelming problems. This workbook describes the twelve most common denial patterns and guides the reader through a series of exercises that help them to identify and more effectively manage their own denial.

The structured exercises contained in this workbook teach the reader how to recognize and more effectively manage their denial when it occurs. Other exercises invite the client to put these new skills to use by identifying and clarifying the problems that caused them to seek help, their life and addiction history, and their personal symptoms of addiction. Clients are then guided through the process of making a firm and deep commitment to taking a next step in recovery.

Denial Management Counseling Workbook *Practical Exercises for Motivating Substance Abusers to Recover*	
Exercise #1: Understanding Denial as a Part of the Human Condition	**Exercise #5:** Stopping Denial as You Think about Your Problems
Exercise #2: Understanding the Principles of Denial Management	**Exercise #6:** Stopping Denial as You Think about Your Life History
Exercise #3: Recognizing Your Denial Patterns	**Exercise #7**: Stopping Denial as You Think about Your Addiction Symptoms
Exercise #4: Managing Denial	**Exercise #8:** Stopping Denial as You Decide What to Do Next
	Exercise #9: Evaluating Your Denial Management Skills

A model treatment plan that can be used to develop practice standards and a sample of an abstinence contract are provided in separate appendixes. A complete explanation of how to use this workbook and its exercises with clients is available in a separate volume titled *Denial Management Counseling: The Professional Guide for Motivating Substance Abusers to Recover.*

HERALD PUBLISHING HOUSE/

INDEPENDENCE PRESS

1-800-767-8181

OR

(816) 521-3015

ISBN 978-0-8309-0850-9 (Workbook)

DENIAL MANAGEMENT COUNSELING PROFESSIONAL GUIDE
Advanced Clinical Skills for Motivating Substance Abusers to Recover
By Terence T. Gorski

Project Team: Terence T. Gorski, Stephen F. Grinstead, Arthur B. Trundy, Joseph E. Troiani, and Roland F. Williams

This professional guide discusses a number of issues related to motivating clients to recover by using a systematic process to manage denial, overcome treatment resistance, identify serious problems, and motivate clients to resolve them. It includes:

Part I: Understanding Denial
1. Learning the Denial Management Systems
2. The Definition of Denial
3. The Levels of Denial
4. Denial and the Human Condition
5. Principles that Govern Denial
6. The Denial Patterns

Part II: Managing Denial
1. Confrontation in the Management of Denial
2. The Denial Management Interactional Process (A Communication System for Stopping Denial)
3. The Denial Management Clinical Exercises (How to Use the Client Workbook in Group and Individual Therapy)
4. Denial Self-Management Training (A Psychoeducation Program for Denial Management)

Part III: Advanced Clinical Skills for Denial Management
1. Avoidance
2. Absolute Denial
3. Minimizing
4. Rationalizing
5. Blaming
6. Comparing
7. Manipulating
8. Consequential Recovery
9. Compliance
10. Flight into Health
11. Strategic Hopelessness
12. Democratic Disease State
13. Denial Strategies

ISBN 978-0-8309-0965-0

To Order Contact: Herald Publishing House/Independence Press
www.relapse.org
1-800-767-8181 or (816) 521-3015